Memoirs of a Solo Traveler

My Love Affair with Italy

By Margie Miklas

For my late husband, Steve,

who loved traveling as much as I do

and encouraged me to go to Italy without him.

Acknowledgments

I would like to express my gratitude to those who were a source of inspiration, encouragement, and support to me during the preparations and actual journey through Italy and the writing about it.

To my late husband, Steve, who always made time for travel, and even encouraged me to go to Italy when he no longer could. Thank you for all the memories.

To my parents, Arthur Longano and Phyllis Longano, who taught me to be proud of my Italian heritage and traditions.

To my Italian teacher, Lori Samarin, who always encouraged me and challenged me to do a little more. You truly allowed me to have the courage to immerse myself into the Italian culture.

To my nurse manager, Cindy Norris, who was willing to allow me to take the three-month personal leave of absence from the hospital to go to Italy.

To my brilliant editor, Almut Metzroth, whose tireless dedication and attention to detail made me a better writer. I am still learning from you, Almut.

To my sons, David and Brian, who never tire of my sharing photos and stories about Bella Italia. And if they do, they never let me know.

To my brother, Rick, and my sister-in-law, Monica, for taking me to Italy for the first time.

To the rest of my immediate family, Mike, Randi, Jim, Christy, Ed, Amy, Katie, Emily, and Candace, and also to my extended family, for all your love and support.

To my friends and family in Italy, Angela, Teresa, Antonella, Calogero, and Monica, who always make me feel welcome.

To my coworkers and friends who continue to listen to me talk about Italy whenever I have the chance.

To all of you who follow my blog and take the time to comment, I truly appreciate your support.

To my readers who touch my heart when you tell me that you feel as if you were traveling beside me.

To the countless supporters on social media. I value your re-tweets and your likes, and even more, interacting with you.

Table of Contents

Preface

The year I turned sixty, two things happened to me. I got contacts for the first time in my life, and I went to Italy for the second time.

Sixty sounded so old, but I didn't feel old. I felt offended when the eye doctor wanted to know why I wanted contacts at my age. I told him, "I may be sixty but I feel like forty." I wanted to try contacts despite what he thought. The more he tried to discourage me, the more of a challenge it became for me, and I was determined to make the lenses work. Two years later I am very glad I persevered and didn't give up.

When I went to Italy in the fall of that year, I went with Sue, a friend of mine. We flew to Rome together and after a few days there, we took a twelve-night cruise all around Italy and then spent a few days in Sicily before returning home. The trip was wonderful, and Sue was very instrumental in my realizing how independent I actually was.

The ship docked overnight in Livorno and Venice. In both ports, Sue decided to stay on the ship the second day and I went ashore on my own. I never felt alone and truly felt at home as I walked down the streets of Pisa for the first time by myself.

During that outing a woman asked me in Italian for directions to the *Campo di Miracoli,* and I surprised myself when I not only understood her but was actually able to give her directions in Italian. I was pleased with myself and at that moment, I realized that I could come to Italy on my own and manage just fine. That was the beginning of what later developed into the experience of a lifetime for me.

As soon as I got back home I knew that I wanted to revisit Italy some day. There never seemed to have been enough time, so I longed for the opportunity to go to Italy and stay for an extended period. That thought never left my mind, and I daydreamed about how I could transform my longing into action. What I did know was that one day I would go back and I would go by myself.

I had not traveled alone before, but the thought did not scare me. I sort of liked the idea of being able to make my own itinerary and plan things the way I wanted. I never dreamed that a year and a half later I would be going to Italy on a solo adventure for three months.

Leaving for Italia

Well, the day has finally arrived. After months and months of planning and researching and making arrangements on my own, I am going to Italy on a solo adventure for the first time. I am all packed and ready to go to the airport, and tomorrow at this time I will be in *bellissima* Venezia! *Io sono molto entusiasta!* I am so excited! I thought I was traveling light by taking one medium bag but it still weighs almost fifty pounds. I will have to drastically reduce the items I want to take as the weight limits on flights within Italy are lower. *Vediamo.* We'll see.

I am excited and also a little nervous, mostly because of the weather. Rain is expected and I am hoping for no delays or I may not make my connection in Atlanta, due to Delta adjusting the flight time. Well this is the start of an adventure, and I am quite sure that in the next three months my life will change. I know I will miss my family but thanks to Skype and Face Time and e-mail, plans will work out. I am also quite sure that not everything will go smoothly, but this is life, and I am ready for it. I realize that I am fortunate to be going on this kind of trip and that I am truly living my dream.

As luck would have it, my flight out of West Palm Beach (PBI) is delayed and despite changing to another flight, that one is delayed too, so my fears of missing my connection in Atlanta have become a reality. I am now booked on a flight out of Atlanta four hours later than originally scheduled. The flight is not non-stop to Milan but instead has a layover in Amsterdam.

The adventure has definitely begun. Gone is my carefully preplanned window seat so I may have a chance at sleeping on this nine-hour transatlantic flight. I guess this is my lucky day after all, ironic as that sounds, because the Delta agent at the check-in gate in Atlanta kindly switches my middle seat to a window just before boarding.

Finally I am on the plane and the flight goes smoothly; I am able to sleep about five of the nine hours. As I am sitting in Amsterdam's *Schiphol* airport, I am trying to figure out the timing and logistics of getting to Venice and getting checked in by the deadline tonight of eleven thirty. I have reservations at the *Istituto Canossiano*, one of the convents and monasteries that I have reserved, and if I'm not there by the deadline the doors will be locked. What a sad state that would be for me.

In the fairly vacant airport waiting area I notice an Italian woman reading a book. I decide to speak in Italian to her, asking her advice about taking the autobus or train to Milan's *Centrale* train station from *Malpensa* airport. She speaks some English so it is easy to communicate. During our conversation I learn that we are arriving in Milan at rush hour, 5:00PM, and the bus is best, although it takes an hour. Apparently the train from the airport goes to a different train station and not the one I need, *Milano Centrale*.

I already know that the latest train I can take from Milan to Venice leaves at 8:00PM, or I will not make it in time. Once this travel day ends, and I am in Venice in my room, I will start to relax and really begin to enjoy Italy. Right now it is a little stressful, mostly because I am worrying about the timing. I am not one who worries that much about things, but when I do, it almost always relates to being late or missing a deadline for something. I'm sure it resonates back to my childhood somewhere.

I know from previous experience that the travel day is always long and seems like a lot of work, but it will be so worth it! I already love listening to the sounds of the Italian language as I wait for my flight with native Italianos. I also truly enjoy being able to understand much of what I am hearing, thanks to my wonderful Italian teacher, Lori.

The past year and half I have taken Italian grammar classes most of which involved private tutoring for two hours every week. I feel as though I can read and write Italian well enough to get by, and I also understand a fair amount as long as someone is speaking slowly. I am able to speak Italian but I think that is by far the hardest because I still have to think about the sentence structure as I'm speaking.

My hope is that after three months in Italy, much of the time being immersed into the culture of the people, I will learn so much more. The reality is that I will be there alone and will have to talk to people if I want to enjoy myself.

Finally I am boarding the plane to Milan and I am once again excited. Not long into the flight I am completely in awe of the Italian Alps as I see them outside my window for the first time in my life. They are huge and it seems as though the plane is not that high above them. They appear to continue for miles, nothing like the Rockies, the highest mountains that I have seen. Like a typical tourist I am going crazy taking photos with my iPhone camera out the plane window.

The flight is short but long enough for me to be able to enjoy the incredible aerial views of the Lakes area of Italy. I am not sure if I am seeing Lake Garda or Lake Como but I am pretty certain it is one of those. I am surprised again by the size of these lakes. They are very large, and naturally, I am snapping photos again.

After landing in Milan and while waiting for my baggage, the Italian woman who told me that there were no direct trains to Milano Centrale finds me and tells me that I know more than she does, pointing to a sign listing the time I had previously researched on my iPad. I guess I know more than I think.

Interestingly another Italian woman comes up to me at the baggage carousel, inquiring if this is *da Amsterdam* (from Amsterdam)? I understand her and answer in Italian! I love this.

I make it in time to buy a one-way train ticket at a cost of seven euros to go to Milano Centrale, from where I will be able to catch the train to Venice. It is late afternoon and warm here. Someone mentions 25 degrees, which is 77°F, quite a bit warmer than normal for northern Italy in the beginning of April. I am not tired yet, and that's a good thing since I still have to take another train and a boat before I can rest tonight.

I am finally on the train to Venice! I just made it! It's dark outside so I can't really enjoy any scenery; besides I now feel very tired. Expected arrival time in Venice is 9:40PM, and then it's a walk to the *vaporetto*, water bus station. I buy a pass and take the vaporetto to the stop closest to my accommodations, and then walk there and check in. By then I will be ready to sleep.

The directions from the vaporetto stop to the convent are *perfetto*, perfect, and even though it is eleven at night, I am not alone as I walk these side streets of Venice. I love the ambience of this neighborhood; I see people strolling along and they all appear happy. At 11:00PM I finally arrive at *Istituto Canossiano*, a convent which is now a guesthouse for tourists and also provides living quarters for students of the Canossiano Institute. Two wonderfully welcoming nuns and a young college-aged man are here to greet me. I am so thankful and happy to see them after my thirty hours of travel on three planes, three trains, and a boat, not to mention the walking.

This place is so peaceful and quiet and has beautiful gardens, and a courtyard that I can even appreciate at night since it is lit.

The atmosphere here is lovely, and I am in Venice enjoying myself and speaking Italian. *Tutto bene!* Everything is good. Now, however, I am going to get some much-needed sleep.

After two full days in Venice I am happy to say that I have yet to step into one museum or church since my arrival. It's not that I don't appreciate museums, but if I have a choice and have a certain amount of time to spend in an area, I always choose to wander around outside, sit at a little café or *trattoria* and just enjoy the sweetness of doing nothing, or as the Italians say, *il dolce far niente*. This concept is a mainstay of the Italian culture.

And so my plans for this trip have built-in times to be able to do just that, since I will be in Italy for three months. I remember that, when I had traveled to Italy before, it was for two or three weeks at the most, and it was never enough time; I felt that I didn't have the luxury of whiling away the hours, enjoying the people around me and slowly sipping a cappuccino with the breeze against my cheek and my scarf wrapped a little tighter around my neck. My love of Italy is always more about the people and the experience of discovering little-known places.

Now on this same thought, it is always a good idea to know of a few museums that may be interesting in case of bad weather such as rain or cold temperatures. It doesn't exactly work for extreme heat since many museums in Italy are not air-conditioned, although they frequently are cooler than the outside temperature due to their stone construction.

Venice is certainly the place for uncovering surprises around every corner because there are no real streets here. It is definitely a walking city, and I am not surprised that I do not see many bicycles, because of the hundreds of little bridges, which must be traversed by steps in both directions. It would be *molto difficile*, very difficult, with a bike. Believe me, it was hard enough with my bag when I first arrived here.

Instead of streets there are some alleys, called *callés*, which are literally only about five feet wide. I understand that somewhere in Venice is an extremely narrow callé that is less than two feet wide at one end. It is a given that I will get lost here, even with a map (which is a good thing to have), but getting lost in Venice is part of Venice's charm, and I have the time to do it with five days here.

A map is a help, but I am learning my own little tricks to help with directions. I count steps to the next turn and take notes on a small pad; otherwise there is no way to find my way back. Even with this technique, I still set out for my intended destination and soon realize that I cannot find my way back without getting lost. Yet some of these trips provide me with views I would otherwise not have seen. Of course, being a photographer, I look at it as another great photo opportunity.

The weather is unseasonably warm here, *fa caldo*, as the Italians say. It feels like late spring or early summer without humidity. What more can anyone want? I totally enjoy being here and particularly love having the time to notice the little things. I observe how relaxed the Italian people seem to be, as they stop to talk with each other over a morning cappuccino and *cornetto*, sweet roll, their typical breakfast. The local people appear to have no sense of being rushed, which is so prevalent in America.

Today I am going to Murano to see the master glassmakers at work. I want to make up for my previous visit here several years ago on a Sunday, a day when most of the furnaces shut down.

I take the vaporetto across the lagoon; after about thirty minutes the boat approaches the island of Murano and I love seeing all the old glass factories from the water. Naturally this is another photo opportunity for me and eventually I get off at the *Murano Faro* stop.

With no pre-arranged tour, I wander around in search of an open furnace where I hope to be able to watch glassmaking first-hand. The first place I stop at is not such a good experience as some businessmen in suits want nothing to do with me and turn me away. They explain that the factory is only open to visitors who have pre-arranged and pre-paid for a tour. Not at all discouraged I keep exploring this small town.

Well, I am in luck because just by chance I find myself at the *Schiavon* Gallery and have the privilege to meet designer *Massimiliano Schiavon*. The very beautiful and welcoming *Livia* cannot be any nicer to me as she greets me in English as though I am some kind of VIP. She gives me the only seat and I am now having a private, personalized demonstration by two artisans! While not really understanding why I am getting the royal treatment here, I am not complaining.

"You came on the right day," she says, and explains that Massimiliano himself happens to be here today and is overseeing two of his master glassmakers, *Claudio Zama* and *Giorgio Valentini*. The men are in the process of creating one of the most beautiful vases I have ever seen. Watching them practice this specialized art, with the hot furnace and brilliant orange flames behind them, is mesmerizing. I am sitting close enough that I can feel the heat on my face.

The friendliness and generosity of everyone in this shop is overwhelming to me. After some time, Livia introduces me to the famous designer, Massimiliano Schiavon. He is young, slender, and has caring eyes. In his pink sweater he looks very attractive. When he stops working for a while to talk with me in Italian—Livia is helping with translation—I am in heaven for this is exceeding by far any expectations I ever had about what I might do in Murano. If I do not do anything else in this town, I will be happy.

And then his buyer, *Sergio*, who speaks both Italian and English, offers to give me a personal tour and explains the glassmaking process to me. The entire experience is nothing short of incredible! The Schiavon showroom looks like, and truly is, an upscale art gallery. I later learn that each piece has been certified as an objet d'art. I will never forget observing these talented artisans at work and leave their showroom totally content.

As it happens, I then wander into the gallery of the famous *Simone Cenedese* and continue to be amazed! He is the glass designer known for the beautiful blue glass star-sculpture, which sits in the center of Murano. His showroom is absolutely beautiful and everything inside is definitely far out of my price range. Despite the fact that I am not buying anything, I think I could stay in Murano forever!

It's now late afternoon and I'm hungry. I guess I am on the Italian schedule of eating so I stop for a delicious meal of *pasta pomodoro*, pasta with tomato sauce, *insalata mista*, mixed green salad, and a Coca Light at an outside table at *Ristorante Dalla Moro*. Not too many people are here since lunchtime is really over, but I just enjoy the atmosphere and notice the beautiful added touch of a handmade glass vase on the table. This unique piece is fashioned into the shape of a flower, with mint green stems and a pale pink rose. *Bellissimo*.

Of course I must shop for some of the wonderful Murano glass jewelry—how could I resist? I buy a few pairs of earrings to take back, some for me and some for gifts. They are very reasonably priced too. If I can find one of the vases that were on the table where I ate lunch, I will buy one for sure. So far, though, I unfortunately do not see any for sale.

I take the vaporetto back the long way, as it stops at the islands of *Burano* and *Torcello*. Thus, I can continue to enjoy the scenery in the lagoon longer.

When I arrive at the *Fondamento Nuova* stop in Venice, I wander back through the winding passageways to the Grand Canal. There, I sit for a while in *Campo San Barnaba,* listen to live accordion music, and enjoy a Coca Light, Italy's version of Diet Coke.

Of course, *la passeggiata* is all around me. I noticed this yesterday around five o'clock, when suddenly the streets were much more crowded with people, including students and lots of mothers with baby strollers. La passeggiata is sort of a wonderful unspoken tradition in Italy, and it really does happen every day in every city and town. People are strolling around the piazzas and streets eating gelato, singing, talking, and walking their dogs. The children are running about and laughing. Everyone seems happy, and nobody appears to be in a hurry. It is such a great lifestyle.

The next morning I get up at six and get ready to take the vaporetto to the train station. How beautiful it is on the Grand Canal at sunrise with few people around, and to feel the cool breeze in the air. The buildings appear different without the sun shining on them from above, and I notice the quiet.

I arrive early at the *Venezia Santa Lucia* train station and buy a round trip ticket to *Udine* for less than twenty euros from the person at the ticket window. Since I am early I decide that I have time to check out the self-service train ticket machine or *biglietto veloce*.

Most Italian train stations have those two options for buying train tickets. Naturally the machines are faster and more efficient but for someone like me they can be a little intimidating simply because I have no experience using them. That soon will no longer be the case now that I have actually practiced on one with no one watching.

Today I will meet *Nerina*, my Italian teacher, Lori's, longtime good friend. My teacher is from Udine, the capital of the Friuli region of Italy. The train ride takes almost two hours with nine stops, and it is fascinating to see row after row of vineyards, both private and commercial. I didn't realize this before, but Friuli is well-known for its wines. I am enjoying all the green landscape and rural areas, with purple flowers blooming everywhere. They look like lilacs and I wonder what they are called here.

I finally am at the train station in Udine and am looking for Nerina, whom I have not met before but I have seen a photo of her. She is not on the platform so I go inside the station and exit the front door, looking around for a tall, slender, beautiful Italian woman. And there she is with a big smile and arms outstretched. This is what I mean when I say the Italian people are wonderful, and I always feel at home here.

Nerina is so friendly and welcoming, as though we had known each other for a long time. Looking like a model in her tailored white shirt and slimming pants, this very attractive Italian woman, who is not much younger than I am, makes me regret not having lost weight before coming here. Nerina is fit and in great shape, a good role model for me for sure. Nerina whisks me away, and immediately the Italian conversation begins. I quickly realize that she knows less English than I thought, and I can see that today will be an extended Italian lesson for me. I am both excited and a little bit nervous.

We get into Nerina's car and she drives the short distance to the center of Udine. It is already warm and sunny as we start our walking tour. Springtime in Udine means many plants are in bloom, especially those strange purple flowers, which later I will learn are wisteria, and in Italy they are called *glicine*. Their prolific blooms emit a pleasant, sweet aroma, a little like lavender, and quite intoxicating.

Nerina explains that all the major buildings here are smaller versions of some of the great buildings in Venice, and I suddenly remember having heard something about this from Lori, my Italian teacher. After a while we stop to quench our thirst and I choose a cold drink called *Ace*, which is sold in a can and is a concoction of orange, carrot, and lemon juice. I like the refreshing taste and it is healthy too.

I realize that Nerina is intentionally speaking mostly Italian to force me to do the same and to challenge me to understand everything as best I can. I bet Lori told her in advance to do this, and for me that is strenuous work. I know that this is the way I will improve my learning the language. This is total immersion.

Now we are driving to the ancient medieval city of *Cividale*, which is the birthplace of my Italian teacher's mother. Cividale is very clean, not crowded at all, and quite charming. This is not a typical tourist town and the only people I see are native Italians. In the middle of the afternoon Nerina suggests we have some lunch. I am caught by surprise, when she points out the *Café Longobardo,* which is well known here for regional food. At a window we order the food and then sit across the way on some stools, waiting for our order to be ready.

We have a little of this and a little of that to taste the food typical of this region: quiche, polenta, *formaggio,* cheese, and *bruschetta,* thin slices of warm toasted bread rubbed with garlic, and olive oil. Nerina insists on treating me as her guest for the day and does not allow me to pay for anything. She almost gets angry when I try to pay and this reminds me of how my Grandma Savoca would act when she was determined about something. Nerina also buys something called *strucchi,* a sweet strudel-type pastry from this region. She sends me back to Venice with it, apparently aware of my sweet tooth, and I do not argue.

Eager to show me some of the historic sites in Cividale, Nerina buys tickets to tour the ancient *Monastero Santa Maria* and the *Tesoro del Duomo,* which are nothing short of awesome.

The entire day is an incredible experience. I have my own local, personal tour guide and host at the *mercato*, market and the walk along the waterfall. Once we cross the *Ponte del Diavolo*, or Devil's Bridge, we can see the snow-capped peaks in nearby Slovenia.

Of course we sample some gelato, do some window shopping, sit at an outdoor table to have coffee in a piazza, and meet some of Nerina's friends who willingly pose for photos with us. Thank you, Nerina, for a day that I will remember forever.

At eight I am on the train back to Venice, exhausted and happy.

Some say that Venice is dirty but I don't find it to be so; instead I find it very appealing as it is so unique and I believe there is no other place in the world like Venice. I could easily come back to Venice again and again.

Staying in the *Dorsoduro* area is wonderful since it is a quiet residential neighborhood and I get to see how the local people live. I am really happy with my accommodations at the convent; it is very peaceful and quiet here.

Today is Sunday and my last day in Venice. Instead of sleeping in as planned, I awake early and may as well take the five-minute walk to *Chiesa San Trovaso* for the one and only Mass offered today. I am one of no more than fifty people attending. The service is uplifting, although the priest is celebrating Mass without the help of servers, ushers, or Eucharistic ministers. Consequently the ceremony lasts less than an hour and, naturally, is presented in Italian.

After Mass I walk to *Campo San Margherita,* where I find a small café and enjoy a cup of cappuccino and a *mandorle crostata,* almond baked dessert tart, as I leisurely sit at an outdoor table. I remind myself that this is exactly what I had dreamed of doing while I was contemplating this trip. This is truly *la dolce vita,* the sweet life! I hear church bells ringing, which is no surprise, because there is a church on almost every corner in Italy, and certainly in every piazza.

While spending my afternoon wandering around Venice with no agenda, I decide to stop in at an Internet café to have access to Wi-Fi for an hour and then wander back to my room. This day of leisure is just wonderful and so much better than my original plan of going to Padua on a day trip. It pays to be flexible.

Later I head to *Piazza San Marco* as this is my last night in Venice. I am intent on finding the same cozy restaurant with five tables that I so enjoyed the previous time I was in Venice. After walking up and down five or six callès, I actually find it! I instantly recognize the red awning, and then I recall the name once I see it, *Anima Bella.* I am thrilled it is open and that there are vacant tables.

The same friendly woman, whom I assume to be the owner, is here, and I am so happy that she can seat me, although later I see that the place is full with reservations. I order spinach tortellini with pomodoro sauce, insalata mista, a glass of red wine and *acqua naturale*, plain water as opposed to sparkling water. Of course everything is delicious!

All of a sudden one of those serendipitous moments occurs. A woman enters the restaurant alone, and the owner is unable to accommodate her at a single table. For some reason I immediately sense some identification with her; perhaps it is her smile combined with the fact that she appears to be traveling alone. I extend an offer to share my table if she cares to join me. At first she declines, not wishing to impose, but I know that if she leaves, she will miss out on a truly authentic Italian experience.

I convince her to stay, and it is amazing that we make an immediate connection, even ordering almost the same food. Like me, she is traveling solo, is from Los Angeles, and is here in Venice to take a mosaics class at the world-famous *Orsoni* studio. We both share the same passion for Italy and laugh and talk throughout our meal, enjoying the time together. What a totally spontaneous fun occasion!

We walk through Piazza San Marco and then go our separate ways but not before exchanging e-mail addresses. Good luck, Cindi, on your Matisse mosaic!

On my stroll home through the narrow callès in Venice I feel so happy and very grateful for the opportunity to be able to be here in Venice on my own with no real agenda. Tomorrow I will leave for *Perugia*. I wonder with excitement what lies ahead.

Going to Perugia

I am leaving for Perugia today so I rise early, pack, and stop by the office to say goodbye to *Matteo*, and pay the remainder of my bill. I will miss him as he helped with Wi-Fi and is the only one here who speaks fairly good English. He is kind and very easy on the eyes too, and one day some young Italian girl will get lucky and find him.

After five days in Venice and riding the vaporettos each day, I know my way around fairly well. This morning I catch the vaporetto to *Ferrovia*, which is the stop for the train station. Venice is so lovely and today is another beautiful warm sunny day. Again I have one last chance to enjoy watching the early morning activities on the Grand Canal, where all the boats carry their supplies to their destinations. The farmers market is already open at *Rialto* and the locals are on their way to work.

At the train station stop I drag my bag up the steps, so grateful that it has wheels and that I have only one bag. The *Frecciargento 9409*, the train for Perugia, is scheduled to leave at 10:27AM with stops in *Padua* and *Bologna* before arriving in *Firenze*. In Firenze I will have to change to a local train to Perugia, which is scheduled to arrive around 4:00PM.

After reviewing the departure boards inside the station, I have no problems locating my platform and boarding the correct train to Firenze. I have the good fortune to choose a seat next to an American on this train to Firenze. It is obvious by his dark hair and his expressed passion for life that he is of Italian descent like me. "I see you are reading some travel books, which are in English," he says. "You must be American. I'm Joe."

"Yes, I am from Florida. So nice to meet an American. I have been in Italy almost a week, speaking mostly *Italiano*. So I am ready to have a conversation in English."

Joe is maybe a little older than my sons. He tells me of his studies in Perugia twenty years ago at the University for Foreigners, or *Università per Stranieri di Perugia*. Today he is in the wine business and tells me that he has been in Verona for *VinItaly*, the largest wine exposition in the world. Every spring, over one hundred and forty thousand exhibitors meet in Verona for this huge event.

Since Joe went to school in Perugia and comes to Italy frequently, he knows a lot about the city and train travel. Of course this is perfect for me to learn whatever I can from him, plus he seems very interesting. The time passes quickly and I really enjoy sharing experiences with someone who has such a passion for Italy. Thanks, Joe, for a memorable train ride and all your tips. I will never forget you.

In Florence I board a smaller train and, as scheduled, at 2:13PM I am on my way to Perugia. By three thirty I notice the hill towns of *Umbria* at *Castiglione* and *Camucia-Cortona*. Umbria, a much less crowded region of Italy, is scenic and very green, just as I had seen depicted so often in paintings and photographs of Tuscany. I wish I could capture these vistas with my camera but I know from experience that a photo shot out of a moving train and through a window streaked with dust and water spots is less than adequate. Therefore, I'm just happy to live in the moment. Not every memory has to be a photograph.

At 4:00PM the train arrives in Perugia. I get off at the second stop, which, I learn from the friendly Italians on the train, is the main station. Once there, I discover that I have to buy a bus ticket and catch the bus to the *centro*, the historic area of Perugia, which sits high above the area of the train station. Thanks to the local students who communicate with me in Italian and a little English, I board the right bus.

Around five o'clock I arrive at my thirteenth-century hotel, *Hotel Fortuna*. After a quick check-in, I unpack and then head up to the rooftop garden to marvel at the spectacular panorama views. I could linger here for a long time but I am eager to explore the city.

At the street level I stroll along *Corso Vanucci* and find myself again in the midst of la passeggiata, of course! Perugia is a very old city but also a college town, so the streets are filled with young people. I like the energy here very much.

Even though native Italians do not eat dinner until eight thirty or nine, I am getting hungry and decide to have dinner at an outside table at *Caffé Perugia*. The focaccia with *rosmarino,* rosemary, and insalata mista sounds wonderful and enough for me tonight. The air feels a little cool but, in Italy, I love to eat outside and enjoy the ambience as night falls. Afterward I head back to my room, do a little laundry in the sink, update Facebook, and relax for the rest of the night.

I am slowly learning that I have to pace myself and build time in to do nothing but relax, il dolce far niente. So today I am doing exactly that. I am so glad to have three months to practice il dolce far niente.

This morning starts with *la colazione*, breakfast, in a beautiful dining room in my hotel. As usual in Italy, breakfast is included with the reservation and it is a full meal, not simply a cappuccino and a cornetto, or *brioche,* sweet pastry, which many Italians eat. I savor this breakfast and especially like the little smiley face that the waitress creates in the frothed milk of my cappuccino. I hardly ever drink coffee at home but I am definitely enjoying it here, as it is so much a part of the Italian culture.

Pleasantly sated, I am back on the rooftop to take in the view once again. Today is a good day to write and update my blog, so I return to my hotel room for a few hours. Later I will do more sightseeing in town.

Walking around, I find *scale mobili*, a series of escalators that transport people from *Piazza Italia* to *Piazza Partigiani,* the location of both the train and the bus station. Riding these escalators I feel as though I am descending into a cave since the historic section of Perugia is perched so much higher than the rest of the city. At the bus station I buy a round-trip bus ticket for tomorrow to spend a day in *Deruta*, about ten miles from Perugia.

This morning I am up at six to catch the early bus to Deruta. I am the only non-Italian on board, and the language I hear spoken must be the local dialect because I do not understand much of it. Every town seems to have its own dialect, which reflects earlier influences.

Arriving early in Deruta, I discover that along with students, I have to take a second bus, to the centro, which of course is perched on a hill, like in Perugia. It is no wonder that in Umbria these settlements are known as the hill towns.

Once in the historic center of Deruta, I begin my exploration of this small town but hardly see any residents, much less tourists. I guess it's because of the early hour. At a little before nine, not much is open yet. In fact, after walking twice up and down numerous staircases, I discover that nothing is open at all.

Eventually I have a conversation in Italian with a friendly woman who indicates that the shops will open soon, and then she is very eager to show me her house and tell me about her family that lives with her. Of course, as is typical in many Italian families, her son, his wife, and their baby son all live together in the mother's house. I can sense how very proud she feels to share her story with me and to tell me that she was born in Deruta and worked with ceramics, for which this town is well-known, the primary reason I wanted to come here. She also wants me to know and see what a beautiful view she has from her home. She is right. In America it would cost an arm and a leg for a view like she has.

This is what I love about being here – this connection with the people. They are all so friendly and hospitable. I am quite sure that she would have invited me into her home if I had kept talking with her. After several minutes I thank her for the information and conversation and resume my walk, feeling a little more secure in knowing that the shops will open eventually. I am certainly getting some good exercise today.

I soon find the small tourist office. The man who works there speaks Italian, German, French and Spanish, but no English. Apparently not too many Americans make this a travel destination. When people say that everyone in Italy speaks English, it does not always hold true in the small towns.

I find I am able to communicate enough with the man in the tourist office to have him understand that I am looking for a place where I could watch someone producing the hand-painted majolica ceramic art. He indicates that I have to go back down the hill to a place called *fabbrica*, a factory. Another local man who is also in the tourist office overhears our conversation and gives me directions in Italian, explaining to me how to reach the fabbrica. I only hope that I can remember this.

Then he leaves the office with me and walks me to a shop nearby, explaining that it is his ceramic shop and that his son works at the fabbrica. Since I am interested in buying some ceramics and I am in a shop that is actually open, I spend some time browsing around, looking closely at all the beautiful pieces. I say to the shop owner, "*Bello, voglio comprare un vaso di biscotti*," or beautiful, I want to buy a biscotti vase. He shows me a very large and gorgeous one, hand-painted by himself and his wife. He turns it over to let me see his name painted on the bottom of the jar. The cost is eighty euros which is definitely reasonable, but after talking for a while in Italian, he lowers the price to seventy euros, and then actually sells it to me for sixty euros since I am paying in cash. This is a great deal and I wish I had a way to carry more items because I would buy more, but I have to be satisfied with this.

The man understands that I have to ship this jar home and, therefore, takes the time to carefully wrap it in bubble wrap. He could not be any kinder. We continue our conversation in Italian, when he tells me all about his family and wants to show me the apartment he owns upstairs, which he rents out for sixty euros a night.

"*La camera é bella, molto bella. Nuova,*" the room is beautiful, very beautiful, like new, I say as he leads me through the apartment of a living room, kitchen, bath, and two bedrooms.

This would be a great place to stay for someone intent on spending time in Deruta. I am beginning to think he may be a little too friendly, though, as he is telling me that when I return to Italy, he will make a *prezzo speciale* or special price, just for me.

Before I realize what is happening, he gently takes my face into his hands and kisses me on the lips, not a lingering romantic type of kiss, but a warm kiss nevertheless, by a strange man in Italy! I am uncomfortable but smile and start making my way out of the apartment as I thank him for showing it to me and also for the biscotti jar.

I hasten to leave for good, but he kisses me a few more times and smiles, telling me in Italian how beautiful I am and calling me *carina.* This well-dressed, attractive man is at least seventy-five years old and I am wondering whether his wife knows that he does things like this. Now I am becoming more uncomfortable and definitely want to leave his shop. Actually, I am ready to leave the historic section of Deruta as well, especially since I already bought the biscotti jar.

I now can say I have firsthand experience with flirtatious men in Italy; it certainly caught me off guard. Every day here is a learning situation. Perhaps this friendliness is just the way that Italians show their appreciation with nothing else intended. Is this all part of the dolce vita?

After leaving the historic center, I surprise myself by remembering how to return to the lower part of Deruta. By asking a few other people for directions along the way, I happen upon a fabbrica where only one lady is inside. I enter and immediately notice the strong scent of paint in the air. I catch her attention and convey to her that I am hoping to see some ceramics being made, although my expectations are quickly dissipating as I do not see any other workers.

To my amazement, this Italian woman gets out her paints and demonstrates for me how she hand paints the images onto a ceramic bowl after transferring them from a template. I can hardly believe that she is doing this with such a fine hand. She informs me with pride that she is eighty-one years old. Totally incredible!

I feel so honored that she allows me to photograph her while she is working. Of course I buy something from her. The price is so reasonable that I also give her five euros extra. She is totally thrilled and her smile is priceless. I leave Deruta very happy.

Back in my comfortable hotel room I have no problem sleeping and before I know it, the morning sun is streaming through my window. I am heading out on another day trip as this is the last day before rain is expected. Assisi is only an hour from Perugia by bus, and the first one leaves at 9:30AM.

When the bus approaches the city, I can see Assisi high on a hill like so many of the other Umbrian towns. What a sight this is from a distance, this grouping of buildings after miles of rolling green hills. The Basilica of St. Francis stands out from its surroundings since it is so huge.

I exit the bus and walk up the hill to the Basilica. There, other visitors are milling around outside. Some of these are in tour groups and I remind myself that I am so thankful not to be a part of that. I prefer going at my own pace and not feeling like I am part of a herd.

Assisi is definitely a tourist town; I see numerous buses, mostly filled with European visitors. I hear very little English spoken. The streets are lined with tourist shops, which takes something away, I think, from the charm and serenity of Assisi.

The hilltop homes are clustered together and the entire area is spotless. Near the Basilica grow shrubs, cut to form the word PAX. Manicured lawns contribute to the tranquil scene. It is so quiet that I can hear the birds chirping.

Inside St. Francis Basilica I am struck by its immensity and beauty. Frescoes by famous artists adorn the walls and the ceilings; many side chapels feature their own frescoes. After wandering around, marveling at all the artwork and sheer size of this church, I visit the tomb of St. Francis. Here I can't help noticing quite a few small photos, apparently placed there by visitors.

The vistas from high on that hilltop are awesome. I walk a lot and enjoy the different photo ops from that beautiful place. As usual, I am getting my daily exercise of hill- and stair-climbing. A few hours here is enough for me, so I take the 1:40PM bus back to Perugia by way of lots of other little small towns I would not have otherwise seen. Because there are a lot of school kids on this bus, the stops include residential neighborhoods, an added interesting change for a first-time visitor like me.

The bus rides through *Torgiano, Bettona, Colle,* and some other small towns before it arrives back in Perugia. Along the way I am able to see mountains with snow in the distance but have no idea which mountains they might be.

By the time I get back to Perugia, it rains. I take the rest of the day to relax, do a little laundry by hand in my bathroom sink, and write.

Since I will be in Italy for three months, I feel like I am living here because I have regular everyday things to take care of, like laundry, writing, paying bills online, checking e-mail, and going to the post office.

I am thinking back to last winter, when planning this trip and trying to figure out an itinerary, I aimed to base myself in towns and allow time to take day trips, buy gifts, and make arrangements to ship them home, as well as schedule time to relax.

A rainy day is a good day to catch up on tasks and errands. I will find out what is involved in shipping a box back home. The post office experience in Italy is a real process to say the least. First I have to take a number, and depending on what my business is there, the numbers are categorized in three different areas. Once it is my turn, I turn in my box along with two documentation forms, which must itemize each item in the box, its value, and the approximate weight. It is not acceptable to simply write gifts, or clothes. After about thirty minutes or so, I leave the post office. Mission accomplished.

On the walk back to Hotel Fortuna I am thrilled to find a *supermercato*, supermarket. I am so happy to be able to buy Coca Light and some other necessities, which are much less expensive there than at any of the smaller shops.

After taking my purchases to my room, I grab a can of soda and return to a little park I passed. I choose a bench and do some writing, enjoying the cool breeze and sun without any more rain.

I will have a late lunch before three thirty, because after that time not much is open until seven thirty, except a bar, that serves minimal items. In Italy most retail establishments and businesses essentially close down in the afternoon and re-open in the evening, so the afternoons become good opportunities for me to relax.

Tomorrow I will take the train to *Orvieto*, another little medieval hilltop town, which is also known for its hand-made ceramics. Orvieto is not that easy to reach without a car and I am sure that the public transportation options of buses and trains will make for an interesting day.

As expected, getting to Orvieto is a two-hour process by itself, beginning with taking Perugia's Mini Metro, three trains, and a *funicolare*, cable car. I hope it will be worth the effort. At the very least, today presents an adventure in Italian transportation modes.

Perugia's Mini Metro, consists of unmanned cars with seats and standing space, each possibly having a capacity for thirty people. This sysytem operates on a series of cables and transports people from the centro storico on top of the hill to the lower part of Perugia, near the train station and other lower areas. The distance it covers is approximately three kilometers, just under two miles, and takes a few minutes at a cost of one euro and fifty cents. It really is pretty cool and in no time I am at the train station.

Inside the train station, while in line to buy my ticket to Orvieto, I meet an elderly Italian gentleman; we have a conversation in Italian about train connections and a *binario*, platform location. I seem to attract Italian men over the age of seventy, because the next thing I know is that he invites me to have coffee with him. I politely decline and quickly make my way to the binario, hoping that he is not taking the same train. I enjoy meeting people and like the chance to practice my Italian, but why does it always have to be old men?

While waiting on the platform for my train, I meet a very nice young, Filipino journalist who now lives in Finland and writes for an online China information site, www.radio86.com. She came to Perugia for the International Journalism Festival and, as a writer, I am very interested in her background. Her

English is perfect when we share stories about the differences between our cultures. Her name is Geni, and we end up sitting together on the train until I have to change trains at *Terontola-Cortona*. What impresses me so is her youth and her accomplishments, moving across the world, learning a foreign language, and writing for a radio station. I have her card and hope to stay in touch with her on Facebook after I return home.

Today seems to be a day for meeting people because prior to the arrival of my train to Chiusi, I meet a Romanian girl, Maria, on the platform. She speaks Russian, Italian, and some English. She is going to visit her friend. When the train arrives, we choose seats next to each other, conversing mostly in Italian until we have to go our separate ways. I never feel alone here, as people are friendly and I like to talk to people. Thank God for my Italian teacher, Lori, who gave me enough encouragement and taught me the skills I would need to be able to communicate in Italian.

Once in Chiusi, I board a train bound for Orvieto and finally arrive a little more than two hours after starting out in Perugia. Perched high on a hilltop, Orvieto is an awesome sight when approached by train. Unfortunately I am unable to get any good photos of that vista from my vantage point on the moving train.

Since Orvieto is situated high up on a hill, there is a funicular to ride to the top at a cost of one euro. A funicular is a railway with a series of cable cars, which are pulled up a steep slope with pulleys. Sometimes it seems like a lot of work to get from one place to another in Italy, and this is one of the reasons I know that I would never want to live here permanently. Like many other Americans, I am too spoiled by the conveniences at home.

Riding the funicular is definitely an experience and I feel as though I am back in time as I hold onto the hanging oval ropes to steady myself. The car I am in is packed with people, mostly young college-age Italians who, like me, are maybe having a getaway from Perugia for the day.

In Orvieto, I walk the winding uphill streets till I reach the highest point, and from there I have some of the most amazing and spectacular views since arriving in Italy. This Orvieto scene is so incredibly beautiful and tranquil!

The immense duomo is the focal point in the piazza. Although this cathedral was built from the thirteenth to the seventeenth century, the prevalent architectural style is Gothic. Huge bronze doors as well as intricate mosaics give evidence of artisanal craftsmanship. A great subject matter for some photos. From there I leisurely wander among the little streets, which have many ceramic shops, as this area has always been well-known for these hand-painted works of art.

After browsing through quite a few, I end up back at the first ceramic shop, where I had   met the smiling and friendly *Chiara Giacomini*, the owner who had spoken with pride of the four generations of her family involved in this *ceramiche artistiche*, ceramic art.

My long-desired plans to purchase some ceramic dishes while in Italy necessitate shipping them home despite the cost. On my last trip to Italy, I was intent on finding a leather jacket in Florence. This time I am definitely coming home with ceramics.

After debating with myself what designs I like best, I buy several beautiful pieces, which actually were designed by Chiara's daughter. Her son *Giulio* is now in the shop helping his mother. He explains to me that he attended art school for five years prior to his becoming the skilled craftsman that he is today. Both Chiara and Giulio carefully wrap my purchases. The added benefit of free shipping is a big plus, compensating for the complex procedures at the post office.

I stop for lunch at *L'Antica Piazzetta* and opt for an outdoor table. This time, I decide to try a regional specialty, fettuccini with porcini mushrooms. Contrary to what my friends may think, I do enjoy other things on the menu besides pasta pomodoro. And the fettuccini practically melts in my mouth.

One of the waiters slices the thinnest prosciutto from a prepared side of pork right in front of me and serves it as a complimentary appetizer. This sample is incredibly delicious. I am surprised, that until now I was never fond of prosciutto. Here I learn that the twenty-four-month aging process makes this product so savory.

Another insight that makes visiting Italy so wonderful. I just do not find these kinds of restaurants with their unique touches anywhere but in Italy. Coming to Orvieto is so worth the effort to get here.

An hour before leaving Orvieto I decide on a whim to do one last thing. I want to check out St. Patrick's Well, also known as *Pozzo di San Patrizio*. This sixteenth-century well was built after the pope stayed in Orvieto as a place of refuge because it was an unsafe time to be in Rome. The well was commissioned in 1527 and completed ten years later by the Florentine architect *Antonio da Sangallo*.

For five euros I purchase a ticket and walk down one of the spiral staircases consisting of 248 steps. The well is 175 feet deep and 42 feet across; it is fairly cool inside. I understand that the immense size of this well is the origin of the Italian saying about spendthrifts having pockets as bottomless as "il Pozzo di San Patrizio."

From a pamphlet I learn that the well had been built with two staircases, one for descending and one for ascending. The steps are wide since they were originally used by donkeys carrying water to the surface. The walls were cut from rock; farther down bricks line the walls. A total of seventy windows are cut into the circular well, which allow light to shine on the steps. The walk down is not so bad; in fact it only takes about ten minutes. Going down is not nearly as intimidating as climbing the campanile in Florence, where one narrow staircase has to accommodate those going up and others going down at the same time.

At the bottom of the well, some water still remains. The air is somewhat damp, with a slightly musty odor. To think that this well was used for the past five centuries is a little eerie. While looking around on the bottom of the well, I meet a few people with whom I share travel stories. We are taking a little break before we make our way back up the 248 steps. The walk up, naturally, takes more than ten minutes.

So far, I find Orvieto is one of the coolest places in Italy.

It is Palm Sunday in Perugia and I am going to Mass at the *Cattedrale di San Lorenzo,* which is only a short walk from my hotel. The cathedral is really beautiful, and as in all Catholic churches on Palm Sunday, there is a lot of pomp and circumstance with a processional today.

One of the most interesting things to me is that on the steps of the cathedral two parishioners are distributing olive branches instead of palms. There is actually a man trimming these before he hands them to those of us entering the church. Since I don't live here and am not going to my home after Mass I don't take a branch before entering the church. In a generous offer the woman sitting beside me in church gives me two of her olive branches. Italians never stop being generous – it is just part of the culture.

The other difference I notice between attending Mass in America and in Italy is that, when the collection is taken, the donations seem to consist of only change. I don't know whether this is the amount that people typically give, or whether previously arranged donations were made. Later I learn that the state collects a church tax from the people and, thus, funds the churches.

On to Siena

Today's travel will take me from Perugia to Siena, another opportunity to learn more about the Italian public transportation system, especially between small cities.

I start out by taking the Mini Metro to Piazza Partigiani to catch the bus to Siena. A sign directs me to the ticket booth across from the train station, but after going there, I discover that at this booth they sell only tickets for city buses and not the regional bus to Siena. The man directs me to a small office behind the ticket booth. I would never guess that this is the place to purchase bus tickets, since it is called Radio Taxi. Another challenge for the American tourist.

I buy the one-way ticket for twelve euros; then the woman directs me to a bus stop, which is supposedly under a bridge near a supermarket co-op. Without too much difficulty I find the place and have a lot of time to spare, particularly since the bus is thirty minutes late. This situation is okay with me. It now provides me with chances to practice my Italian with a woman who is going to visit her ninety-six-year-old mother.

Eventually the bus arrives and it is much nicer than the city buses. This one resembles a charter or tour bus, which is great because it is not crowded, plus I can stow my suitcase   in a luggage compartment and don't have to drag it up the bus steps and find a spot for it.

I can't help myself but I am staring at the bus driver who strongly resembles George Clooney. Taking the bus to Siena today definitely has some added perks.

After a ninety-minute bus ride I arrive in Siena and easily locate my hotel, *Hotel Chiusarelli*. I unpack, grab some lunch, and start exploring. Even though I am no longer in Umbria, the towns still sit on hills here in Tuscany, and Siena is no exception.

Whenever I set out on foot to take in my new surroundings, I know I am benefitting from the exercise. At the same time, I am able to appreciate new discoveries. One of Siena's most famous landmarks is the immense *Piazza del Campo*. Every summer the *Palio*, the famous horse race known throughout the world, attracts thousands of fans to this location. The Campo, as this huge piazza is called, is a terrific place to people watch and relax, and a gelato is just the thing to complement my first outing in Siena. After browsing around the piazza, I sit down and write in my journal, pleased with the peace and tranquility that I feel, and just soaking up the atmosphere of Siena.

It is seven and I am awake, thanks to the loud clanging bells at the nearby Basilica of San Domenico. After a fine breakfast in the hotel dining room I am out and about early to look around

Siena and to locate the bus station in *Piazza Gramsci*. I will take the bus in the days to come to make day trips to *Firenze, San Gimignano, Montepulciano*, and other parts of Tuscany yet to be decided.

Following two and one-half hours of absorbing first impressions of this city, I think it's safe to say that I walked off my breakfast.

On another beautiful sunny day in Siena, as I sit beneath a shade tree in the garden of my hotel, I write down additional details and thoughts of my solo traveling.

I really love having the time to amble around and not having to rush, taking photos and living the moment. Every time I pass one of the large organized groups with a leader holding a flag and reciting lectures, I am thankful I am traveling alone. I like the freedom to do whatever feels good at the time, and with no time constraints. I am reassured that traveling solo definitely has its advantages. I love this experience!

This afternoon I will take a side trip to *Chianti* and go on a tour of two wineries, thanks to arrangements made yesterday through the front desk at my hotel. The tour sounds like a fun time, and Chianti is one of the places I have on my loose itinerary for Tuscany. Why not blend a little fun with education?

At two o'clock Marco from http://www.mytours.it is here to pick me up in his van. I see that I am joining seven others from New Zealand, Brazil, and Boston. They should be good company. Marco informs us that the plan is to visit two family-run small wineries in the Chianti province, one in *Sant' Appiano* and one in *Castellina in Chianti.* Customized arrangements are more personal than presentations to large tour groups.

Located halfway between Florence and Siena, Chianti is a major wine-and olive-producing area in Italy, and the only area where the *Sangiovese* grapes for the authentic *Chianti Classico* wine are grown.

In Sant' Appiano, a very small village, I noticed only a few homes and not many more residents. Centuries ago it used to be the estate of the esteemed *Pitti* family—of the Pitti Palace in Florence. Now it is a small winery that produces approximately 90,000 bottles of wine each year, which are sold only in Italy. Since olive trees are also abundant in this area, Sant' Appiano produces its own extra virgin olive oil as well.

Once we arrive in Sant' Appiano with Marco, we see Barbara, the very friendly owner already outside with arms outstretched to warmly welcome our group. Very shortly her brother and co-owner, Francesco, joins us in the wine cellar. Both Barbara and Francesco speak English and are eager to explain the process of making wine.

Not only do they provide us with a complete explanation of how their wines are produced, but, afterwards, they treat us to a tasting of three of their wines and, to our surprise, even include some of the most wonderful appetizers to go along with the wine. They could not have been nicer. Their family has been producing this wine for the last fifty years, and they know wine!

I am so thrilled that I am here—what an awesome encounter this is for me.

Before we leave, I purchase several bottles of wine and olive oil and arrange to have them shipped home. I guess I will be hosting a wine party after I get back.

For our next stop, Marco drives our group to the town of Castellina in Chianti where we visit *Casamonti*. This is a larger family-operated winery on 350 acres. Here the owner, Anna Rita, and just five helpers produce wine, olive oil, organic spices, as well as cured meats from a specific type of pig called *Cinta Senese*, which is raised only at Casamonti. I find it incredible that all of this work is done by only a few people. They have 3000 olive trees and I learn that olives from five different types of trees go into the production of olive oil. The olives are harvested during the cold months of November and December, both by hand, and only recently, also by machine.

Anna Rita gives us the grand tour of Casamonti. It is obvious to me that she is used to doing this on a regular basis and seems to enjoy it. In her tour of both the outside and inside areas, she includes an upfront and personal look at their home-cured sides of prosciutto hanging in freezers. I can still see the hooves of these pigs.

The tour itself is amazing, but afterward Anna Rita brings us to a large room where there is a beautiful table set for us. I cannot quite grasp this level of hospitality and everyone involved seems so happy to be doing whatever they can for us.

Anna Rita's right-hand man, *Alessandro*, begins to pour three different wines for us to taste, two Chiantis and a Merlot blend. Anna Rita had prepared some bruschettas made according to her mother's recipes, and besides that, the plate holds several other appetizers, including Tuscan bread with olive oil, tomatoes, and some other treats, which I do not recognize but are quite tasty. The food is delicious and complements the wine well. After leaving, I certainly do not need another meal for the remainder of the day!

Casamonti, like Sant' Appiano, does not export its wines outside of Italy, so I think this is really special to be able to taste wines that I will never be able to find anywhere else.

On the way back to Siena, although it was not actually a part of the tour, Marco takes us for a short visit to the tiny village of *Monteriggioni,* where only fifty-two people reside today. The settlement and the castle appear as they did 800 years ago.

On my "to-visit list" are several Tuscany places, Monteriggioni among them. I can now cross it off the list, thanks to Marco. Our group's detour is a perfect ending to a wonderful day in Italy, one of my favorite ones so far.

I arrive back at Hotel Chiusarelli tired. I appreciate that my home for the next ten days is such a beautiful place in the historic part of Siena. This is a comfortable accommodation with ambience; it always waits for me while I take day trips to the little towns in Tuscany.

Hotel Chiusarelli is a nineteenth-century villa, which became one of Siena's first hotels and was recently restored to maintain its original neoclassical style. It is centrally located so the traffic makes it noisy, but the back has a beautiful patio garden and I love to go there to write.

The other appealing feature of this hotel, for me, is that it is the location of part of the story of the New York Times bestseller *Juliet* by Anne Fortier. As a writer I feel a little bit connected to this hotel and inspired to write.

I decide to go to Florence tomorrow instead of today. Due to yesterday's walking tours, my legs want a rest. They do not mind a short stroll, though, to Piazza del Campo, where I can write a little, take some photos, and people watch.

Sitting in my private, personal spot under the shade tree in the garden of *Albergo* Chiusarelli, I couldn't ask for better weather. The mornings and evenings are cool; during daytime it is sunny and warm. At this time of year the hotel does not use heat or air, so the room is a little cool at night but that is a small price to pay for being in Italy.

Wherever I go I notice that the Italians always dress well; even when it is warm, women wear scarves, and sometimes the men do too. Even the police are dressed well in what I learned are Pucci-designed uniforms. If anyone wears shorts and a T-shirt, you can be sure the person is not Italian. Most Italian women as well as men carry crossover bags.

It is not even nine in the morning and I am already on the express bus from Siena to Firenze. Upon checking train schedules I find that the buses from Siena to Florence take less time than the trains, so I travel again by bus today. It actually turns out to be a good move as the trip takes a little over an hour, and the views of the Tuscan countryside are just like I had seen in movies and on post cards. Bellissima!

There are plenty of rolling hills with lush green pastures that seem to go on forever. The golden fields are beautiful and I enjoy a feeling of serenity while watching from my bus window. From time to time I can see those tall Italian Cypress trees that are so quintessentially Tuscan. I wonder how they could grow so straight and get to be so tall without falling over. I also find myself wondering who maintains all of this property.

In Florence I exit the bus station and discover that it is in very close proximity to the train station. This tells me that it will only be a short walk to the Duomo. Based on my research, without a doubt the Duomo, also known as Basilica di Santa Maria del Fiore, is the most compelling landmark in Florence and I know that I want to climb to the top of the *campanile,* bell tower, this time, to make up for a missed experience on my first visit to Florence.

On the way to the Duomo I happen to spot a tourist office and decide to go inside to procure a map, always a convenient aid to have in Italy. Even though I vaguely remember how to get around in this completely walkable city, I have concluded that a map still comes in handy. That is not to say that I still won't get lost, as my explorations in Venice are a prime example.

In less than ten minutes I approach the famous Duomo. I am impressed by its Gothic architecture and take some more photos. One can never have too many photos, I think. Thank God for digital cameras. Eventually I buy a ticket to climb the campanile, which is also known as Giotto's Bell Tower. It is 276 feet high and there are 414 steps.

Once inside I started to climb the spiral staircase with other tourists and hope that this isn't a mistake. I am not in the greatest shape since my weight gain, which I had not lost as I had hoped prior to coming on this trip. I am determined, though, to climb to the top; I am counting the steps as I climb so I can sort of gauge my progress.

At the bottom the steps are about thirty inches wide. At the higher levels they become much narrower as the staircase spirals. There is only one staircase, so visitors use it to ascend and descend, necessitating that everyone might have to stand sideways at times to allow a group to go in the opposite direction. Thank goodness it is April and not July or August, or the heat would be unbearable in this crowded space.

There are several levels where I am able to stop and walk around to catch my breath. I really wish more than ever that I had lost weight because I am now breathing much harder than when I climbed to the cupola of St. Peter's four years ago. This climb is definitely strenuous. Even young people are huffing and puffing and sweating by the time they reach the top, which makes me feel a little better, knowing that I am not the only one who finds this climb to be a challenge. On the last sixty or so steps, people who are descending offer words of encouragement to those of us still going up the stairs. A sense of camaraderie prevails with this venture.

Once I finally arrive at the top, however, the climb was so worth it. The views are just majestic and I can see all of Florence below and also the surrounding countryside. It is truly spectacular! And unlike the Leaning Tower of Pisa, where there are very strict time limits and the authorities monitor the visitors to have ten minutes or less at the top, I am able to spend as much time up here as I want. You can imagine that I am going crazy with my camera, taking photos from all sides. I love being up here, feeling the breeze and enjoying the view from so high above the city. Yes, everyone who is physically able and comes to Florence should do this climb at least once.

Back on the ground, I make my way to the *Ponte Vecchio*, Florence's famous bridge which is lined with jewelry shops. I am on a mission to look for a particular type of cameo for my daughter-in-law, Amy, but I am not having any luck. I look in every single shop and even ask one of the shop owners to bring a few pieces from the safe so I can choose from those. "All the jewelry comes from one place," she informs me in English.

"Do you mean that if you do not have this particular cameo, I will not find it in any of the other shops on the Ponte Vecchio?" She nods apologetically.

At lunchtime I stop at a marvelous restaurant named *Reginella*. It is near *the Accademia* and has a sign featuring a margherita pizza and Coca Light for the unbelievable price of eight euros, a special. This sounds perfect for me, so I find the host and say, *"un tavolo solo,"* a table for one. I think I'm cool, speaking Italian, but the truth is that Florence is so touristy everyone speaks English.

As I sit at my table for one, I notice the waiters and how much fun they are having interacting with the attractive young girls who pass by. The young male waiters make me laugh, as they eye all the young girls that walk by. In typical Italian style, the waiters call after them, *"dove sei stata tutta la mia vita?"* Where have you been all my life? The girls smile at the waiters but keep walking. The determined young waiters smile and shout to them, *"Non si preoccupi. Io non sono sposato,"* Don't worry, I'm not married. They speak very good English and I joke with them about their flirting, and they tell me in Italian that it is a hard job but someone has to do it. They really know how to have fun at work and the whole process is amusing to me. So for eight euros not only do I get to enjoy a great meal but also have some good, free entertainment. I give them a nice tip when I leave and pay them a compliment as I speak with the English-speaking owner. "*Grazie mille, Signore.* I really enjoyed myself. You have some great waiters working here." I can tell that he appreciated the positive words, looked toward his waiters, nodded, and smiled.

After lunch I take time for some serious shopping at the San Lorenzo market. Having been here before, I know that I can find quality leather bags and silk ties at great prices, so I have a lot of fun for the next two hours, and buy everything I need and then some! The vendors are very nice and not at all pushy. If I buy more than one item, or offer to pay in cash, they are glad to make deals. I leave here a happy shopper.

I could spend even more time browsing but I have an agenda that includes making time to visit a nearby hilltop town, thanks to my friend, Tamela's, advice. "You must see *Fiesole*, which is not too touristy, and from there the panorama views of Florence are striking."

So I make my way to *Piazza San Marco* where the number 7 bus leaves for Fiesole. Once there, I double check by asking some young girls, who are waiting at the stop, "*È questo l'autobus per Fiesole?*" Is this the bus to Fiesole?

"*Si, si acquista il biglietto sul bus.*" Yes, you can buy a ticket on the bus.

By four thirty I am on my way to Fiesole, paying the two euros for the ticket. Frequently I am able to buy tickets on the bus but not always. Usually a tobacco shop sells the tickets for a lower price but since I don't have time to find the *tabaccheria*, the extra price is worth the convenience.

After a twenty-minute bus ride to *Piazza Garibaldi* in Fiesole, I quickly find the signs pointing to *via San Francesco*, which leads to a lookout and the best views of Florence. Thank you, Rick Steves, for this information and for warning me about the steep climb. Via San Francesco is an extremely sloped hill with an angle of at least thirty degrees, but it really seems more like forty-five.

Again, for the second time in one day, I wish I had lost weight but I will go up the hill, no matter what. To my relief it is only a ten-minute walk with stops to catch my breath. What makes the climb even harder is that I must carry a bag with all my purchases from a day of shopping in Firenze! How smart is that? Not.

No matter how hard the climb, the views are totally worth it. At five o'clock I am sitting in a public garden near the top of the hill. Church bells are ringing, birds are chirping, and I feel a cool gentle breeze against my cheek, as I look at all of Florence from high above. It is an extraordinary sight with the red tile roofs and the lush green fields from surrounding Tuscany. What a nice oasis away from the faster pace of Florence.

Siena, Soccer and Vino

My plans for today were to do nothing except a few errands, but now it's not even ten and since I have finished the errands, I think I will go to San Gimignano. Whenever I think back to taking that twelve-night cruise around Italy in 2009, I remember hearing so much about this town from other passengers who went there on excursions. So I decide now that during my time in Tuscany, I visit San Gimignano. Besides, on this gorgeous day my feet don't hurt as much as they did last night after walking in Firenze all day. Rain is expected tomorrow, so today looks like a good opportunity to visit San Gimignano.

I am already familiar with Piazza Gramsci, which is the place from which all the buses depart and only a short walk from my hotel. I guess I blend in well because, once again, an Italian *signora* asks me for directions. It seems to happen every day, and I begin to feel as if I were a native Italian, a feeling that I like.

Soon the bus arrives and takes me away on another Tuscan adventure. As usual, before arriving at destinations nestled in hillsides, I get a glimpse of them but can't photograph the idyllic scenes from the moving bus. I must remember to buy a postcard with a view of San Gimignano from far away. San Gimignano is a walled, well-preserved, medieval town located high on a hilltop. Its walls date back to the thirteenth century and some of the cobblestoned streets and piazzas go back to the ninth century. Originally the walls included seventy-two towers of which only fourteen remain; yet San Gimignano is still known as the town of beautiful towers.

Inside the gate I really enjoy walking through this fascinating town, which attracts tourists but is not crowded. It is small enough that I can wander around without a map, discovering new views around each corner. Certainly this place is a photographer's dream and I take advantage of my independence as a solo traveler, skipping from one picturesque scene to another.

Of course the streets are steeply inclined and after wandering around for a while, I find the one which leads me to the highest point in San Gimignano, *Rocca e Parco Montestaffoli*; when translated, it means fortress and park of Montestaffoli. This delightful and serene hilltop park displays rows of olive trees and fields of wildflowers. From here I have a panoramic view of the Tuscan countryside, which can take my breath away. What a wonderful place to sit, rest, and just savor the atmosphere.

After walking back down into the town, I enter a street lined with lovely shops. I find the prices to be reasonable. In fact, I feel drawn to buy a few things, such as a ceramic olive oil jar for my son Brian, who is quite artistic. In one shop I see paintbrushes in a container off to the side of the counter and realize that the ceramic items are made and hand-painted right here.

I love buying things that are authentic, sometimes difficult to find in the States. After my shopping adventure in Florence yesterday, I will make another trip to the post office anyway, so there is no reason to limit myself here. I am so glad I decided on this day trip to San Gimignano. Now I know why people talked about it so favorably.

It is early Friday evening and I am back in my hotel room in Siena. Suddenly I hear a lot of noise outside as though someone is giving directions over a loudspeaker. Today is Good Friday in Italy, so I wonder if an outside religious event is going on at the cathedral around the corner. My curiosity gets the best of me. I grab my jacket and leave the hotel to see what's happening, not wanting to miss out on what could be a major event. To my naiveté and surprise, the cathedral appears to be closed, yet the streets are filled with people and quite a few police. I notice that the people are not strolling as in la passeggiata but instead seem to have an agenda, and suddenly I understand the announcements.

I can see the lights of the soccer stadium, which is directly behind my hotel, and after inquiring from the police, I become aware that tonight a soccer game between Siena and Venezia is on the schedule. Never having been to a professional soccer game, I make a snap decision to go and look for a ticket booth. If tickets are reasonable, I will attend. Fortunately for me, a ticket costs only eight euros, which is incredible. I am quite surprised that I need to show my passport to purchase the ticket and I don't have it with me. It is in the hotel. After a few minutes the ticket seller feels sorry for me and she lets me buy the ticket anyway. Maybe I don't look like a security threat. The other person selling tickets, however, has to accompany me to the gate and explain to the man there that it is okay for me to gain entrance. Again it is a process here to be admitted to a soccer game. I thank the employees, grateful and happy that I can now experience my first Italian soccer game.

Italians are passionate about life but they are really fanatic about soccer! I have always heard about this passion but now have a chance to see it firsthand. I love being part of the crowd, hearing the fans singing, yelling, probably swearing in Italian, and stomping their feet on the aluminum stands, which is making a deafening sound. I have a great time! I'm smiling and nodding to the people sitting near me, whether I understand everything they say or not. I feel a part of it! Not feeling the need to stay for the entire game, I make my exit after about an hour and walk to a gelato shop to end the evening with an amarena, black cherry gelato, a perfect finish to a great day. What could be better than this, I ask myself. I am a very lucky person.

Today, Easter Sunday morning, I have breakfast in my hotel with some Americans I had met previously here. For Pasqua, Easter, a plate of cut chocolates graces the buffet table along with the normal breakfast foods. What a nice **touch**.

After breakfast I go to nine o' clock Mass. The San Domenico Church is just a short walk away. There is no pomp and circumstance, no choir or music, nothing to appear different from any other Sunday Mass in Italy, and I am amazed at the stark contrast between Easter Mass here and in the U.S.. One hundred people are in attendance in this large church and no woman wears a hat or fancy clothing.

The entire Mass is presented in Italian, but since I have attended thousands of Catholic Masses in my lifetime, I know exactly what is going on and pray silently in English. The Italian language is not that much different from Latin, which was always spoken at Mass when I was a child. Not until Vatican II in the early sixties was Mass in America was changed to English. Again I notice that when the collection is taken, the donations consist of mostly coins. I understand now that in Italy, like in Germany, the churches are supported by the state, and the citizens are taxed accordingly.

I do find it interesting that quite a few people have brought small covered baskets with eggs, or chocolate, or bread and place them on a table at the entrance to the church. After Mass, when these apparently have been blessed, the people retrieve them to take home. I think it is a fitting tradition but I see it for the first time.

I plan on relaxing today, so after Mass I go out for my daily exercise and walk to a small park near Piazza Gramsci, where I notice two swans in a small pond. I spend some time here, enjoy the atmosphere, watch the swans, and take photographs. This scene feels very peaceful to me. After some time alone here I head toward the Campo, which I know will be crowded. All the restaurants have special Easter meals with *agnello*, lamb. Nothing on the menu appeals to me since I don't like lamb. So I just browse around and decide to have lunch somewhere else. On the way back toward my hotel, I stop in at my favorite outdoor restaurant, *Il Masgalano Ristorante Pizzeria*, across from San Domenico Church, and order pasta pomodoro. It may not be the typical Easter meal in Italy but I am happy.

Easter Monday is a holiday in Italy as the Italians know how to extend the Easter holiday to include Monday, or *La Pasquetta*. Official offices and many shops are closed and the trains and buses run on a limited schedule. Most Italians spend the day away from their homes, having picnics in the park. I remember my Italian friend, Angela, describing this holiday to me, explaining that most Italians go to the countryside on Easter

Monday. For this reason I decide to go back to Florence rather than Montepulciano. To reach that city requires several modes of transportation. I have a mission in Florence: to return to the San Lorenzo market and purchase more silk ties, per request from my oldest son, David. By now I know how to get there without any problem, and I find the ties right away.

Afterward, as I am casually strolling along the streets of Florence near the Ponte Vecchio, just by chance do I discover *Rossopomodoro*, which is an excellent chain restaurant that originated in Naples, Italy. Recently two of these restaurants opened in the States, one in Naples, Florida, and the other in the mega mercato, Eataly, in New York City. I am both surprised and excited to find Rossopomodoro and talk to the waitress about the fact that there is one in Florida. She speaks English and I am a little disappointed not to be able to speak Italian. I have an excellent lunch here, and no, it is not pasta pomodoro but my other favorite, margherita pizza san Marzano. I am not a foodie, and am not that adventurous when it comes to trying all different regional foods, just because I am in Italy. I could actually eat pasta pomodoro, margherita pizza, and insalata mista every day, because it is always so well prepared.

My mission accomplished, I am soon on the bus back to Siena. On the way home from the bus stop, I get soaked in a heavy rainfall, but it doesn't matter since I am just returning to my hotel. Eventually it stops raining, and I go back out for la passeggiata. A little more exercise can't hurt, especially after the pizza. Tomorrow I will get up early and visit one more hill town, Montepulciano, where parts of *Under the Tuscan Sun* and *The Twilight Saga: New Moon* were filmed. I am looking forward to it, even though it entails taking two buses and a train to get there.

I know that reaching Montepulciano will be chaotic and time-consuming today. Since Tuscany is a region of hills, there frequently is no easy way to approach some of these small towns that sit on top of a hill. This is why all the tour books suggest seeing Tuscany by car, but since that is not an option for me traveling solo, buses and trains will have to suffice. Montepulciano is the highest of Tuscany's hill towns at almost 2000 feet elevation. Walking the inclined streets here is not that bad and I think I am just becoming used to it. The weather is cool, perfect for walking. Even though I recognize that tourists are here, it certainly is not crowded, just how I like it.

One of Montepulciano's claims to fame is its wine, specifically the *Vino Nobile*. It doesn't take long before I stumble upon *Cantina Contucci*. I remember reading in Rick Steves's book that the cellar master, *Adamo Pallecchi*, is frequently on the premises. He has been making wine for over fifty years, and to my delight he is here. This elderly man with a full head of white hair, a wonderful smile, and a twinkle in his eye is conversing with a few patrons as he pours glasses of wine for them. He is very engaging and personable with anyone who enters his wine cellar, welcoming me with a smile and a *"Buon giorno."*

Although others are already tasting his Vino Nobile, Adamo wastes no time pouring some for me to try. He appears genuinely pleased that I am here. We have a conversation in Italian about my reading about his cantina in Rick Steves's book. After hearing this, he is even more charming and kisses me. Yes, another Italian man over the age of seventy. I am coming to realize that this is part of the way they show their pleasure over meeting someone. I may be getting used to this.

Afterward I wander around *Piazza Grande*, keenly aware of the fact that this very place is where Diane Lane watched a flag-throwing contest in *Under the Tuscan Sun*. A more recent film, *New Moon*, of the Twilight Saga series, was also filmed in this piazza, although I see absolutely no signs of commercialization of either of these films here. Montepulciano has a clock tower in this piazza, and after paying the nominal one euro fee I start the climb to the top. Within a few minutes I can go no further and am disappointed to find there are only twenty-six steps, so it really is a piece of cake. It seems like there should be more steps for as high as the tower appears to be. The steps are very rickety, and actually they end at the platform. The higher section of the tower is never open, I am later told. I am sure it would be too dangerous, if the lower steps are any indication.

At lunchtime *Caffè Poliziano* is the perfect spot to enjoy some more Vino Nobile and a good meal. This is one of the oldest restaurants in Montepulciano, and is full of character. At this busy time I have to wait for a table, which gives me an opportunity to check out the pastries in the case.

After a delicious meal, I am back on the bus by four o'clock for the hour-and-fifteen-minute ride to Chiusi, where I catch the train back to Siena. For someone who is used to driving a car every day in my normal life, I am learning to be flexible when relying on public transportation. By the time I get back to Siena and Hotel Chiusarelli I have been gone thirteen hours, and all but four consisted of riding in a bus or a train, or waiting for a bus or a train. But it was so worth it!

You thought, I tell myself, you had the post office figured out but apparently not. This morning I go there to buy a box, and obviously I am in the wrong line, because after I finally reach the window, the clerk matter-of-factly informs me in Italian that there is another area where a signora will sell me a box. When I go to wait in line in that area, I happen to be behind a man who needs some research by the clerk in several volumes of binders. After at least fifteen minutes here, and no concern by the clerk that I am patiently waiting, I finally am able to buy the box, and then go back to my hotel and pack it. This is just the way it is in Italy at the post office, *molto lentamente,* or very slow. This first trip there takes over a half hour. Then when I return, after waiting in line again for another twenty minutes or so with my packed box, I discover to my dismay, that the box weighs over five kilos, and now I will have to pay quite a bit more. Not anticipating this, I only have fifty euros in cash, and, naturally, credit cards are not accepted at an Italian post office.

I admit that I needed to go to a *Bancomat*, ATM, today anyway, and I guess I should have gone prior to the post office errand. The result of poor planning on my part now necessitates my leaving the post office, finding a Bancomat, and returning to pay the eighty euros shipping price. Not only is it a production to ship something home but it is expensive. At the current exchange rate of $1.43 to the euro, the fee for my parcel amounts to $114.00. I know it's outrageous but it is what it is. I think I will curtail some of my shopping so that I can minimize my trips to an Italian post office in the next few weeks. Life in Italy is frequently much slower than in the U.S., and sometimes this is definitely part of its appeal. When you live here though, you have to deal with this every day.

The shaded terrace at the back of my hotel is such a peaceful setting. Surrounded by lush greenery planted in terracotta pots, I am sitting alone out here, writing and listening to the birds twittering. It is a little cool, and I hear some traffic from *Viale Curtatone*, the main street in front of my hotel. I am having a home-made lunch of fresh Tuscan bread, pecorino cheese, Italian cheese made from sheep's milk, and a pear. And everything seems perfect. There is a great food store called *Consorzio*

Agrario not too far from here where I was able to make these purchases. All their take-outs are freshly prepared there.

This is my last day in Siena, and I have already made three trips to the post office. I am catching up, packing my belongings. I may go down to the Campo one last time this evening. I will be leaving for Rome in the morning, which requires a bus and two trains. Siena is not on any direct routes to many places other than Florence, yet it has been a wonderful city to base myself in for my ten days in Tuscany without a car.

Next Stop Rome

Across from the train station in Siena is an indoor shopping mall, something new for me to see in Italy. I have a little time before my train departs so I browse around and check out a shoe store. After walking in Italy for the past three weeks, my feet are killing me, especially my right foot. By not bringing any athletic shoes, I hope to fit in with the Italians and have some form of shoe fashion. Lots of Italians wear athletic shoes, however, and maybe that type of shoe will be more comfortable for me. I try on a pair that are distinctly European and similar to what many young Italian girls and women wear. Good, I think, these sneakers are much more comfortable than what I have on and the price is reasonable. I buy a pair and wear them out of the store. Now I will have more to ship home later, but what matters is that my feet don't hurt.

At the terminal I board the train for Rome and arrive at *Roma Termini* at 3:30PM. I find a taxi and give the driver the address for the convent where I will stay during my time in Rome. If this convent is anything like the one I stayed at in Venice it will be great. I had hoped to find one closer to the Vatican, but with the beatification on May 1, I am lucky that I found lodging. The hotels' prices are sky high, adjusted to the demand; a convent or monastery, is therefore, perfect for me, at a fraction of the going rate. Who cares if I have to walk a couple of miles to the Vatican? I am here for a once-in-a-lifetime event, the beatification of Pope John Paul II.

The taxi ride seems to be taking a lot longer than I expected, which makes me a little uneasy. The street for the convent is *Via XX Settembre* and I ask the taxi driver to drop me off at number 3, although this building does not look anything like a convent. After entering the building I find out that this place is not a convent at all. I show my papers to the Italian gentleman inside, and I ask, "*Via Settembre numero tre, un convento?*"

The gentleman peruses the documents rather quickly, shakes his head, and explains to me that I am at the wrong address. "*Questo è il numero tre. l'indirizzo è il numero sessantotto.*" I realize that the correct address is actually 68 and not 3.

"*Dove?*" Where, I ask. The kind man walks outside with me and points down the street in the same direction from which I arrived with the taxi. "*Grazie mille, Signore.*" Thank you, sir. So my walking exercise is starting out earlier than I had expected, since the convent is about a mile away and I am backtracking with my luggage to number 68. I could have walked from the Termini but what else can I do now but hike to number 68?

At my destination a nun greets me. The sisters at the convent speak only Italian, so I am glad that I can speak and understand enough to have a conversation. My accommodations are much different from the luxurious hotel I had in Siena, but the place is clean, safe, and includes breakfast. The gardens look inviting and pretty, but first I want to unpack and explore Rome for a while .

I head towards *Trevi Fountain*, and no matter how often I see it, I love to come here again and again. There is something magical about Trevi. It is always crowded and everyone seems happy. Of course I toss a coin over my left shoulder, keeping up the tradition that ensures I will return. Eventually I get away from the crowds at the fountain and continue my explorations of Rome on foot. As luck would have it, I get caught up in la passeggiata on *via del Corso*, one of the busiest streets in Rome. This district is familiar to me since I rented an apartment near here during my first trip to Italy with my brother, Rick, and his wife, Monica.

I find my way to the *Pantheon* and enjoy some dinner at an outdoor restaurant while appreciating the busy atmosphere. I like being in the city, but it is a little of a culture shock after all those small towns in Tuscany and Umbria. The meal here is nothing special, and I presume the reason is because I am in one of the most touristy parts of Rome. Many Americans are here and I hear English spoken all around me.

This morning, after a great night's sleep, I am up early and leave out the front gate of the convent, headed toward the Spanish

Steps. I expect to have the opportunity to shoot some great photos with fewer people at this time of day. The majestic, magenta-colored azaleas are in full bloom and the air is filled with their perfume-like fragrance. I can't ask for a better time to be at the Spanish Steps.

After my photo shoot, I stop at *Caffè Greco*, which is Rome's oldest coffee bar and has been in existence for 250 years. Since breakfast at the convent consists of only Melba toast and espresso, I am feeling hungry and order my first *cannoli* since I arrived in Italy. I take the cannoli to go because there is an additional ten euro charge to eat it here. Unfortunately for me, I don't realize it now, but I later learn that I could have eaten the cannoli inside without the extra charge if I didn't sit at a table. Of course the pastry is delicious, and worth every penny of the six euro charge because I am in Rome and having a cannoli from one of the best cafés around.

As I continue my walk and approach the Vatican, I notice all the *carabinieri*, police, and media setting up for Sunday's beatification of Pope John Paul II. *Piazza San Pietro* is crowded as I would expect from my earlier visits. The size of the crowd is nothing compared to what it will be this Sunday, I am sure. I understand from *Sorella*, Sister, Emma at the convent that the people are supposedly starting to line up at midnight on Saturday night. I consider my option not to go to St. Peter's Square on Sunday, and instead be part of the faithful watching the event on one of the big screens around the city.

After wandering into the Vatican gift shop I purchase two items I had promised to buy for some coworkers. One is a rosary and the other is a medal of the Sacred Heart. Everything in the Vatican gift shop has been blessed by the Pope and that is why I am buying these items here instead of down the street where they are probably less expensive. My mission here is accomplished, and I do not feel the need to stand in line to visit the Vatican today. I walk away from St. Peter's Square and back into the city of Rome.

My next stop is *Campo de' Fiori,* and, to my amazement, I am able to find the little bar, which I want to revisit. I remember tasting the best *biscotti* here during my trip with Rick and Monica four years earlier. I still search for this same type of pastry with its unusually strong almond flavor and thick crunchy texture and chocolate frosting. I am thrilled that the same signora is inside, and when I show her a photo from four years ago, she is visibly amazed too. The place looks exactly the same, untouched by time, with the same kind of biscotti in the same spot in the case. We have a conversation in Italian and I buy some biscotti and take another photo, giving her the earlier one. I really like connecting with someone from my first trip to Rome, not to mention finding the biscotti again!

Later I stop in at *Forno Campo de' Fiori* and watch as the pleasant Italian bakers make the bread and the pizza. They are only too happy to pose for a photo for me, after which I continue my walk till I reach *Piazza Navona,* which is close by. This large oval-shaped piazza is a perfect place to take a little rest and listen to some live jazz music by street musicians before I head back toward Via XX Settembre. On the way I stop in at an internet café. It does feel so good to get off my feet. After five hours of walking Rome's cobblestoned streets, my feet are definitely in need of a break.

It is now late afternoon and I rest in the peaceful garden at the convent, which is a welcome scene after my day of ambling all over Rome and the Vatican. The gardenias are blooming and their strong, sweet fragrance is unmistakable. I like to listen to the melodic, chirping messages of the birds. This is a great place to write.

When I return inside the convent, I spend some time conversing with Sorella Emma, who is young and so kind. As we talk, she corrects my Italian and I continue my Italian lessons as I go. I share with her some of my photos from my trip and she seems to enjoy seeing my stops along the way.

"Tomorrow I will be busy. Many more visitors will arrive here," she says in Italian, "*Domani, molte persone arriveranno qui.*" It is clear to me from her gestures and the intonations of her voice that she recommends staying away from the *un milione*, one million, expected at St. Peter's. I thank her for the information and explain that tomorrow I may decide to go to Santa Maria Maggiore Church, which is nearby.

It is now Saturday morning, and after spending the evening mulling over the pros and cons of going to the Vatican for the beatification at noon today, I still am not sure what to do. For now I want to find an internet café, so I head outside early before the expected intermittent rains start, and walk a mile toward *Piazza Barberini,* where there are many more shops. Locating a small place which advertises internet and Wi-Fi, I enter and pay a few euros for internet access. Here I check e-mail, update my blog, and post some photos on Facebook for an hour. I walk back to my room in the rain, and catch up on some writing and do some laundry by hand.

Afterward I go out once again to walk around the city and visit some landmarks. The rain has temporarily stopped. I feel cold and damp and keep looking for Mr. Sun but he isn't going to show. This weather reminds me of Ohio with the grey skies and no sun for days on end. I am glad that I went to the Vatican yesterday.

I am getting used to all this exercise because I walk all over Rome again and before I realize it, another three hours have gone by. I have no specific agenda, so I walk past *Piazza Repubblica* to the Forum, the Colosseum, and *Santa Maria Maggiore* church, one of the locations where a large screen stands erected for the public to watch the beatification tomorrow. Videos of John Paul II are already playing and people are quietly standing in the piazza, watching. It is awesome to see so many people outside in Rome, yet the atmosphere is exceptionally quiet. I am quite certain that I will come here tomorrow morning, since this place is only about a thirty-minute walk from the convent. By now, thirty minutes of walking feels like nothing.

On my way home I stop in for Mass at a small but beautiful church on a street not far from the convent. Thanks to Sorella Emma, I know there is a Mass at six tonight.

After the service, on the recommendation of two Italian ladies leaving church, I stop in at *Caffè Piave* across the street and order margherita pizza and a glass of red wine. The seating area is covered overhead so the on-again, off-again rain does not matter. It is early. There are only a few people besides me at the tables outside. Over dinner I find myself people-watching again. My attention is drawn toward a group of Italian men having drinks together, laughing, and talking. I wonder how they know each other. The camaraderie is apparent.

I think I will be ready to leave Rome tomorrow, as I prefer the smaller towns in Italy. In just a few weeks, though, I will return here, when my brother and sister-in-law join me. So I don't see the need to tour the Colosseum or any of the other buildings, because we will probably do that together later. Moreover, I will be glad to leave the convent. I don't feel comfortable here because my room is so damp. It is located in the basement, and at first I thought the sheets just didn't dry enough, but after replacing them, the situation remains the same. The room is very dark, and the recent rain seems to compound the problem of the dampness. I will not be recommending this place to anyone, for sure. More rain is in the forecast.

We'll see how close I get tomorrow morning to be a part of the crowd watching the beatification from Santa Maria Maggiore.

Today is Sunday, May 1st, 2011, and this is the day of the beatification of John Paul II. I am eager to witness the event but not quite sure what I will encounter in the way of crowds, so I am up early and walking the thirty minutes to Santa Maria Maggiore. Although rain is expected again, so far the weather is cooperating and today is a stark contrast to yesterday's grey and wet conditions. The streets are quiet, although I am still two miles away from the Vatican, where I am sure there are already hundreds of thousands of people.

To my surprise and joy I am part of the first group of people to arrive at the site at Santa Maria Maggiore and am able to get a spot very close to the large video screen, maybe twenty-five feet away. Now I feel even happier that I made the decision to come here instead of fighting the crowds at St. Peter's. An aerial video shows on a big screen the wall-to-wall people at St. Peter's Square. That totally reinforces my decision. I have a great seat on the ground in front of the screen and feel a part of spectators who share my spirit of wanting to be here for this historical event.

During the entire time of waiting, the crowd stays very controlled, as everyone is here for the same purpose. Nobody is pushing anyone to get a better spot and everyone is respectful. It reminds me a little like having lawn seating at an outdoor concert, minus the marijuana and alcohol, but the mood of the people is much more somber. The security personnel are even handing out bottled water at no charge. Unlike all the vendors set up in the area around St. Peter's, there are absolutely no signs of commercialization at Santa Maria Maggiore. I am among those who want to celebrate the beatification of their beloved pope, joined by others who are attending this historical event.

I am extremely moved and inspired to be part of thousands of people of different nationalities, participating in the Papal Mass and beatification of John Paul II. I sit near a large contingent of people who traveled here from Poland. They are very passionate in their love of this pope who hails from their homeland. I am especially touched by their reactions, by their applause and flag waving, and their undivided attention. It is apparent just how much this means to them.

I am thankful I can be at this ceremony. It does not matter that I know no one here or that I did not come with anyone. I am involved in something that is really hard to describe. I am surprised to be so emotionally affected by the ceremony.

Watching it live is very moving and at times I feel that I cannot stop the tears from falling down my cheeks as I feel so proud to be a Catholic. Being here brings back all the nostalgia and memories from my youth and my Catholic education and upbringing.

During communion I am surprised to see about fifteen to twenty priests emerge from Santa Maria Maggiore Church to distribute Holy Communion to the crowd during the Mass. I had been wondering about that and assumed that none of us would be able to receive Communion since the Mass we watch is taking place two miles away at St. Peter's. So this is a real blessing. I think the applied logistics and planning for this huge event are proving themselves successful today.

The ceremony lasted about two hours. Now it is a beautiful, sunny, warm afternoon and definitely too nice to be inside. I check my map and figure out how to get to *Borghese Park*, which is sort of the Central Park of Rome. It is huge and includes the famous Borghese Museum and Gardens. I will visit that park for the first time and since my lodging is in that section of Rome, I want to take that opportunity.

I find a shady spot close to the entrance where I can spend some time relaxing, writing, and listening to the Black-Eyed Peas on my iPhone. I am intrigued watching several men who are engaged in a heated game of Bocce Ball. Nearby sprawled out on the grass, friends are having picnics, dogs are playing, some on leashes and some not, and people are riding bicycles. It is springtime and the park's flora is green and beautiful. I prefer being away from the city noise and the always busy Rome.

Incredible Carrara and Bologna

"Arrivederci, Roma!" I leave Rome today and expect the trains to be crowded after the beatification yesterday. A lot of the tourists are probably heading home. May 1st is also Labor Day in much of Europe. This holiday typically draws several hundred thousand people into Rome. Well, there is a limit to how many events I can attend.

At Rome's Termini station I buy my ticket to Carrara. The only option is a ticket for standing room only. If I don't buy this ticket, the next train does not leave for three hours and that will then involve one or more changes of trains. So I now have a standing-room-only train ticket to Carrara. This should be interesting.

Lucky me, I find a vacant seat as well as a spot for my luggage just behind me. Of course, if someone claims this seat, I will have to stand. So I hope that fortune is on my side in this intercity train, IC, which is scheduled to arrive in Carrara four hours after departure from Rome. The train is definitely full; several people argue about seats, but no one appears to have my number so I just remain quiet. If necessary, I would say, "*Non parlo l'italiano,*" I don't speak Italian.

When you travel to small Italian towns that are not typically tourist locations, you are sometimes the only one alighting from the train. And that, as we finally reach my stop, Carrara-Avenza, seems to be the case. I try to open the train door but nothing happens, no matter how many times I try, and there is no one to ask for help. I do not have time to walk through to the next car with my luggage, so I have no option but to watch as the train departs the station, and I ride it to the next stop, La Spezia.

While riding to La Spezia, I notice a sign beside the door that says "*Porta non funziona*," door is not working. This would never fly in the States. I have since come to understand that this situation happens regularly on some of the Italian trains. In fact, Rick Steves suggests departing the train from the same door through which you enter. That way you know for sure that the door will open. This good advice I will heed from now on.

In La Spezia I have to buy another ticket to return to Carrara. Of course the train authorities are not at all interested in the fact that I could not open the door, but they gladly sell me another ticket to Carrara. At least it is the middle of the day and not the last train at night, so the adventure continues. The good news is, the sun is still shining, it's warm, and I'm excited to go to a place that's new to me.

I am staying at the Hotel Michelangelo in the center of Carrara, a complete 360 degrees from the damp, dark convent in Rome. I am in heaven in this modern hotel, which is beautiful and spacious, about three or four times larger than my last lodging. It feels so good to be sleeping in a big bed, have room to move around, and a shower not only big enough to turn around in but made of marble.

I already love being in this little town of Carrara. I speak Italian with locals walking their dogs, while we stroll in the piazza. Everyone is very friendly and seems happy to take the time to talk with me. They seem fascinated by the fact that an American is in their town. I see only locals here.

Then I discover a *Bolle Blu* self-service Laundromat a few blocks away from my hotel: I will finally have the luxury of doing my laundry in machines. It feels so good to have clean clothes again. Somehow they just don't seem to get as clean when I wash them by hand in the sink.

After inquiring at the front desk I make arrangements for a tour to the marble quarries. At eleven Gianni, the tour guide, picks me up in the lobby of my hotel to drive me to the quarries. He is young, friendly, and attractive. He speaks English, explaining that everyone here has to take English in school, so most young people speak it fairly well.

Once we get as far up the mountain as we are able to go in his car, we are met by his friend who runs Carrara Marble Tour. This friend drives us in a four-wheel-drive vehicle the rest of the way to the top of the *Fantascritti* quarries 6000 feet above sea level. The S-bends in the road are not for the faint of heart. I don't know what I was expecting but I am completely blown away by the enormity of this area. I had no idea just how huge these mountains of marble are. There is no question of ever depleting the marble supply of Carrara, the largest quarry of white marble in the world and the actual place where Michelangelo obtained the marble to sculpt his famous David.

This marble basin is only one of three, and supposedly the other two are wider. "There are over twenty square kilometers of marble in these mountains," Gianni explains in English,"and the marble runs even deep beneath the sea here." Incredible!

In these operating quarries the labor involves an intensive process and is an awesome sight to watch. It is understandable why the price of marble is so high, although the pay for the nearly 200 or so quarrymen working in each basin is not considered to be that good, Gianni tells me.

Following my touring the quarries I opt to visit one of the caves where the marble is extracted from the interior of the mine. On this tour I ride in a jeep along with some others almost half a mile to the middle of the cave, and at that point we are a quarter mile beneath the surface. The informative guide explains that Carrara owns the mountains and allows corporations and individual owners to operate quarries, for which they must pay a fee based upon the weight of the marble extracted from the mines. In addition, they must comply with the Italian governmental safety regulations or risk losing their ability to operate.

It is fascinating to me that I am in the exact spot where the car chase scene in the 2008 James Bond film *Quantum of Solace* took place. Gianni points out a demolished building, which appeared in the movie. "The quarries were closed for two months to film the ten-minute scene," Gianni says. "Can you imagine that cost to the filmmakers?" After riding on these roads, I clearly realize why stunt drivers are paid so well.

Gianni's friend operates a small gift shop at the entrance to the quarry. After the tour I buy something to drink, browse around, and decide to buy a set of grey-and-white marble salt and pepper shakers. They are beautiful and the price is reasonable. Now I have a perfect memento from my incredible day in Carrara. Not many visitors to Italy come to see this place; I am so glad my plans include a visit to this town. When it is time to return to the hotel, Gianni is ready to drive me back down to the center of Carrara. What a great experience. I love this!

When I return from the marble quarries, I grab a quick bite to eat and then take a bus to *Marina di Carrara*, the next small town with a port and a beach. Away from Florida, I miss the beach. So it is wonderful that today I can sit on a piece of driftwood on the wide and mostly deserted beach and feel the breeze on my face and the sand between my toes. I can smell the salt in the clean air, and as I listen to the rhythmic sounds of the waves, I can see the blue Ligurian Sea in front of me. If I turn around, the majestic mountains, gleaming with white marble, rise behind me. I always feel so relaxed and peaceful whenever I can be near the ocean. Bellissima!

After a good night's sleep I am out walking the streets of Carrara and checking out all the shops. The Carrarese people are so nice. They will leave their shops and walk halfway down the street to give directions. While I am in a gelato shop, having my almost daily dose of this amazing dessert, a group of young teenagers hears me asking for directions. Since they know some English, they understand what I am asking, and they are all so eager to help me. They actually leave the shop with me, all six or seven of them, and excitedly walk me all the way, at least two blocks, to show me where I need to go. It must be a sight, half a dozen Italian teenagers, boys and girls, leading me down alleys and hills in Carrara. This is so much fun.

On my last evening in Carrara I discover a wonderful little osteria called *La Capinera*. An osteria is a restaurant that usually serves wines and simple Italian food. I am not sure this place is open, but it has these funny string-like door coverings down the front entrance through which I am able to see inside the restaurant. There are a lot of small tables and no people, but the door is open, so I go inside. It is early, six thirty. Of course no Italians are eating dinner at this time. But I am hungry so I hope I may be in luck and be served. Tonight I really am hungry for some pasta pomodoro.

Soon a pleasant gentleman appears. I assume he is the owner. He is only too happy to seat me and bring me a menu. I am the only one in his restaurant and I feel like a VIP. He brings me some bread. I do not see pasta pomodoro on the menu but I ask him, "*Vorrei pasta pomodoro, per favore?*" I would like pasta pomodoro, please.

With a smile, he nods and says, "*Pasta pomodoro. Certamente, per lei, signora, io prepararlo.*" Pasta pomodoro. Certainly, for you, Madam, I will prepare it.

How great is that? A meal cooked to order by the owner of the restaurant. I realize that there is no one else working in the kitchen. I can hear him prepare my food and really feel like a special guest in his restaurant! What a treat, and of course, *tutto buono*, everything is good.

The following morning I am on my way to the train station via a crowded city bus. A young Italian man gives me his seat, and this initiates an emotionally charged conversation in Italian between him and an older woman. I would gladly give her the seat, but it is very clear to me that he is making a point that it had been his seat, and he gave it to me. I don't dare get involved with this heated Italian exchange. Italians are really polite and helpful to strangers, and also very passionate about things that are dear to their hearts. This instance shows just that.

When the bus stops at the train station, I get off, and this same man unloads my bag for me, walks me across the street to the station, and lifts my bag up the steps. He is such a gentleman and not seventy-five years old either.

I arrive early at the train station in Carrara because I want to buy my ticket to Bologna, my next stop on this awesome solo adventure in Italy. I will have to change trains only once, in Florence. After my ticket purchase I have time to wait, look around, and notice how small the Carrara-Avenza station is. Everything is made of marble, naturally, including the seats outside, the walls and floors of the waiting room, and even the steps going to the different tracks.

Across the railroad tracks I can see the mountains looming high into the sky, gleaming in the sun. This beautiful place in Italy most Americans never see. I soak it all in and feel blessed to be here. Now it is on to Bologna, and maybe the towns of Ferrara and Ravenna. Vediamo. We'll see.

My accommodations in Bologna are not in a monastery or convent, but to my surprise, *San Tommaso* is actually a college, and guests stay in the dorm. Students still live here but on a different floor. My room at San Tommaso is much more pleasant than the convent accommodations I had in Rome. The friendly Italian woman at the desk speaks English.

"The curfew here is at 1:00AM," she says. "Your room is on the second floor." She hands me the key and directs me to the elevator. I have a great view of the neighborhood from my window, and I already like Bologna.

I set off to explore the city and find *Piazza Maggiore*, which seems to be the center of activity. A lot of students and young people in general pass by me, because Bologna is home to the oldest university in the world, dating back to 1088. Today enrollment counts are over 100,000 students.

Bologna is easier to get around in than Rome because the streets appear to be laid out in a more organized fashion. What makes this city unique is the number of porticos extending over the sidewalks. I probably will never need an umbrella because so many walkways are covered. Some of the porticos are actually works of art with frescoes on the ceilings. The architecture here is also magnificent, and around every corner is another *palazzo*, or building. On this, my first visit to Bologna, I really survey this city, which has a population of half a million people.

Bologna is known as the gastronomic capital of Italy so I must taste the food here. A charming outdoor ristorante called *Bistro 18* on *via Clavature* captures my interest, and I decide to have dinner here tonight. It is early so most people are having drinks and appetizers for the *aperitivo* or cocktail hour and I am hungry for a pizza. I know that I am in the food capital here, but not being a foodie, I am just as happy to savor the taste of pizza instead of something more exotic.

On the walk home someone stops me and asks me for directions once again and I realize that I can give them in Italian. I have some cryptic notes for myself, so I may find my way back, and I actually know where I am. I must look like I belong here, because the reaction when I say *non solo Italiano*, I am not Italian, is one of surprise.

While walking home I contemplate my day tomorrow; I might take the train to *Ferrara*.

The strap on my luggage is broken, so this morning I go to the ferramenta or hardware store, and buy a *dado* and *bullone*, nut and bolt, and a small screwdriver. In this typical, small store a shopkeeper is happy to find exactly what I need to repair my luggage myself. Life is simple sometimes.

Afterward, on my way to the train station, I pass Bologna's famous two towers, known as *Le Due Torri*, and I also come across a *manifestazione*, demonstration, apparently against Berlusconi's policies. Italians are passionate about everything, and this reminds me of the sixties, when young people in America were so involved and passionate about their beliefs concerning the war in Vietnam, civil rights, and feminism. I feel inspired to see Bologna's many students and young people in general, so involved in a cause.

The train ticket to Ferrara costs only four euros. Forty-five minutes later I arrive in Ferrara. After walking fifteen minutes to the center of town, I locate the tourist office and obtain a map, always a good resource to have when exploring a city on your own.

One of the map's indicated sights is Ferrara's famous castle, complete with a moat. I check it out and discover that *Castello Estense* dates back to the fourteenth century. This huge castle is not crowded by tourists, so I meander around and wonder what life was like here seven centuries ago. I can't really imagine struggling every day to secure a livelihood in primitive circumstances.

Soon I am back on Ferrara's streets. Quite by accident I come across the well-known osteria *Al Brindisi*, the oldest osteria in the world, dating back to 1435. Travel guidebooks highly recommend this restaurant for authentic food from Ferrara and mention somewhere that Copernicus once ate here. Naturally, since I am hungry, I decide that my lunch will be here, and I may be brave and try something other than pasta pomodoro.

Interestingly, in Italy a restaurant can be called a *trattoria*, a *café*, an *osteria*, or a *ristorante*. Today many of these names are loosely used but originally an osteria was a place that served wine and simple food at a modest price. Today its menus are usually still short with more emphasis on local or regional specialties. Like at Bistro 18, the tables are shared. In general, osterias are open in the late afternoon and evening. I understand that some of them serve only drinks and allow patrons to bring their own food.

Even though Bologna is known as the gastronomic capital of Italy, I read in a travel guide that Ferrara has even better food. I want to try some regional cuisine here, so instead of my favorite pasta pomodoro I order what the waiter recommends, their traditional *pasticcio di maccheroni alla Ferrarese*, a macaroni pie with a green salad and some wine. While I wait for my food to be prepared, I meet a young American student named Kellen, who attends the University of Bologna. He is about twenty years old, comes from California, and is very friendly. We have a nice conversation, and he gives me a few suggestions on places to check out in Bologna, particularly *La Sorbetteria* on *via Castiglione* for the best gelato. I remember that my son, David, as well as travel books, mentioned this gelato establishment. So La Sorbetteria is now on my to-visit list.

My meal is served and the macaroni pie is so delicious. The complimentary bread that accompanies the meal, however, is not at all tasty. Unlike anything I know the bread is baked into a hard, unusual, twisted shape, sort of like an x. I am surprised that in Ferrara, of all places, the pane is so tasteless. My thought that this must be a local specialty turns out to be correct, because recent information tells me that this bread is Ferrara's famous *Coppia Ferrarese* bread. Not only is this staple considered to be a specialty of the region but it has PGI, or Protected Geographical Identification, recognition from the European Community. There are strict rules governing the preparation of this bread and over 300 Ferrarese bakeries produce it daily.

Another very helpful tip I learn from Kellen, and who better to know about this than a college student, is the Italian tradition of aperitivo. The aperitivo is a drink before dinner, usually several hours before, along with some complimentary snack food, such as chips, nuts, and olives, or a full spread including salads, bruschetta, pizza, fruit, cookies, and nuts. The aperitivo is also a chance to socialize with friends, and when don't Italians like to do this?

Until I met Kellen I always wondered how the Italians could be hungry for dinner after this aperitivo hour. He educates me on the practice of using this aperitivo as a meal replacement, explaining that for as little as five euros, he could have a drink and pizza and this would be his dinner. On a college student's budget this is perfect. Thank you, Kellen, for this practical lesson, which I will implement immediately. It works well for me since I do not like to eat dinner at nine like the local Italians.

Ferrara is really easy to navigate on foot. You would have to try to get lost. One of the tourist-recommended buildings in Ferrara is the Palazzo *dei Diamonte*, or Palace of Diamonds, not named because the building houses diamond jewelry, but for the shape of the stones on its façade. Now, that I stand close to it, I can understand the rationale. Approximately 12,600 small pink and white pyramid-shaped stones comprise the outer walls of this palazzo. The building is unique, impressive, and the first monument or structure that I face with this type of design. Today this fourteenth century building is an art museum, the *Pinoteca Nazionale*. Right now it happens to be closed for lunch.

Since the shops also close in the afternoon until four, I look around the streets of Ferrara for a while before heading back to Bologna on the train.

In Bologna, just outside the train station, I happen to notice a poster indicating the transportation strike, which is scheduled to occur at 7:30PM tonight, so I am lucky to get back early enough to avert that potential problem.

Today I need a break from walking around towns filled with palaces, museums, churches, and castles, so I am taking the train to Rimini to go to the beach. And in Rimini I don't want to waste time figuring out which bus goes to the beach. Instead, I take a taxi, which also gives me the chance to practice speaking Italian on the way there. The driver was born in Rimini and speaks no English, so it works out well. My Italian teacher, Lori, would be so proud of me.

The beach is my favorite place to be, and Italy is my second favorite. That combination makes for a perfect day. The sea is absolutely beautiful. The color of the water of the Adriatic is blue, but in varying shades. A breeze brings a salty taste to my lips. The sand here is brown on this very wide beach; the seashells consist mostly of black clam shells. For four euros I have a beach lounge chair for the rest of the day and I feel like I am in heaven.

Rimini's beaches go on for fifteen to twenty kilometers and are very popular, especially in the summer. I'm lucky the season hasn't yet started, because the beach is not crowded, even though this is a weekend. After I completely relax for a few hours, it is time to leave. I locate the bus stop after asking the locals a few questions and quickly figure out which bus to take back to the station. I opt for this choice rather than the taxi. No Italian practice for me on the bus, but the ride costs only one euro, much less than a taxi. Rimini is very lovely and I'm so glad I came, even just for part of the day. It was so worth it.

The train ride back to Bologna, however, is another Italian lesson for me, this time with two Italian women. I enjoy being able to converse with them in Italian, as they speak no English. When they understand that I am an American traveling by myself in Italy, they seem to think my adventure is pretty cool. Their smiles and nodding back and forth to each other say it all.

Back in Bologna, I grab a cab to *Piazza San Domenico*, so I can be in time for the six o'clock Mass.

After church I stop in at *Caffè San Domenico* on *via Garibaldi* for a panini with salami, which the bartender makes to order for me. For dessert, my heart is set on some gelato and I know just where to go. La Sorbetteria Castiglione is the best gelato shop in Bologna and I enjoy my cone while walking back to my room. Tomorrow will be a busy day starting with an early nonstop train ride to Verona

Random Thoughts

On to Verona and Milan

After being in Italy almost five weeks, I find that certain habits and traditions seem to be part of the Italian lifestyle and are quite different from what I am used to in America. Some of these random observations may be common knowledge to others, but many are new appreciations I am gaining of the Italian culture.

Tables in almost every restaurant are usually set with wine glasses, as it is the preferred drink at meals. This is not typically seen in America except at high-priced restaurants or Italian restaurants in places such as Little Italy in New York City. In most restaurants and trattorias, all the waiters are men.

Italians think nothing of eating gelato or pizza, as well as drinking wine, early in the morning. Most Italians have caffè after dinner, and in fact whenever I decline, a waiter always reacts in complete surprise. Drinking soda with meals is definitely not a common practice, and there is no such thing as free refills either.

No matter how warm it is, most Italians are wearing scarves, and this custom pertains to men as well. They dress in multiple layers and often wear boots. Italian women wear very high heels, called stilettos, and manage to walk with no problems on Italy's cobblestoned streets. As my Italian teacher, Lori, explains, it is all part of the *bella figura*, or looking good, and the Italian people take pride in their appearance.

Many Italian bus drivers do not seem to be interested in helping you know at which stop to get off, or even whether the bus is going to the location you want. They frequently seem to be more interested in talking on their cell phones. This depends on the particular town, though, and can't be said for all of them.

These are just some of my random observations in a country that is not my home but is my heritage, and I love it. I am definitely enjoying this chance to spend three months here and get to know the people. I am sure that not all of my impressions hold true for all parts of Italy or for all Italians, of course. During another five weeks I will certainly learn even more about the lifestyle of today's Italians.

It is now time to leave Bologna and start the next leg of this adventure in Verona, a city located between Venice and Milan. My taxi driver is only too happy this morning to converse with me in Italian, another chance for me to practice it on the way to the station. I recognize my improvement in the language, because we have a conversation the entire way, ninety-five percent of which I can understand. He, in turn, seems to understand what I am saying in his language, so all is good.

My preparations for my effective communication on this solo trip included grammar lessons with a small group for about six months and one year of private instruction with the same teacher, Lori.

"It's not enough to know the basics of a language but also the way the native speakers think and live," she always stresses. Her advice per se enables me to speak Italian this length of time here.

At noon I am in Verona. My truly beautiful hotel is *Hotel Accademia*; its location is perfectly situated in the center of town. After I unpack I head out to *via Mazzini* and *Piazza delle Erbe*. The piazza is like something out of a movie, with its outdoor restaurants and well-cared for buildings constructed of marble. The streets of Verona are paved with pink marble, which is quarried not far from here. There are all kinds of trattorias and osterias, as well as little shops and boutiques that line the piazza. To me, Verona is one of the most beautiful cities in Italy, and I immediately sense that I am going to enjoy being here.

After some lunch at one of the outdoor trattorias, I am off to find the famous balcony of Juliet, which is always crowded with tourists. The building dates back to the thirteenth century and is said to be the house of the fictitious *Giulietta Capuleti*. I am content seeing the outside rather than going inside the house for a fee. There are so many people here that I can't get a photo of the balcony without someone peering out from that spot.

The famous bronze statue of Juliet is in the courtyard, which has lines of visitors who cannot wait to have their photos taken as they put one hand on her breast. This tradition is supposed to bring good luck; I don't feel the need to follow the crowd. All I want is a photo of the statue without people, and eventually I am lucky enough to capture one.

All along the courtyard walls are hundreds if not thousands of locks left there by lovers over the years. These locks are a common sight in Italy and it speaks to the passion Italians have for romance. I leave there rather quickly, smiling to myself.

Next, I head over to the oldest monument in Verona, the Arena, which was built in the first century and is a smaller version of Rome's Colosseum, but this one is completely intact. Today the Arena hosts operas and concerts and can seat 20,000 people. This amphitheater is in fact the largest outside opera venue in the world.

I am amazed to see this ancient arena in the middle of a city, sitting at the edge of *Piazza Bra*. Open for tours, the Arena charges a reasonable fee, so I purchase a ticket to explore the inside of this Verona landmark. Eager to have the best view, I climb the red steps up to the top, trying my best not to fall. These steps are quite steep and all I need is to injure myself here.

Trying to imagine what it would be like to be here in the summer for an outdoor opera performance, I am intrigued as I watch what is going on today. Some workers are setting up the stage for an upcoming musical event and I assume it will be awesome in these surroundings. This ancient arena, some of which still has the original marble, is centrally located, so people have easy access.

Another landmark in Verona is the *Ponte Pietra*. This structure is an old Roman arch bridge dating back to 100 BC, and crosses the *Adige* River. With its five arches of varying sizes the bridge is a beautiful sight.

In Verona I can easily walk almost everywhere and see the main sights, but since I have a few days here, I decide to buy a ticket for the Sightseeing Verona Hop-On, Hop-Off bus. The ticket is good for twenty-four hours and well worth the cost, because I know I would not have seen some of the places just by walking. I find it interesting to learn a little bit of history about Verona, especially the fact that until 1866 Verona, as well other parts of northern Italy were under Austrian rule. The city is surrounded by heavy walls, which were used to fortify it from invasions over the years.

One of the best lookouts is on the other side of the Adige River, at the highest point in Verona at *Castel San Pietro*. From this altitude, I have a panorama view of all of Verona, which looks like a postcard. I am thrilled with this splendid photo opportunity that I simply cannot pass up.

After the bus returns to the center of Verona, I wander back to my hotel, have a light lunch outside next door at *Caffè Scala,* and afterward board the bus again to see more of Verona. The weather is perfect and between the bus tour and my city map I have a good idea of where interesting sights are in Verona.

I can't help but notice that unlike every other Italian town on my tour, in Verona there are no clothes hanging out on balconies anywhere. I wonder if there might be a local ordinance banning the custom in this city, one of the wealthiest municipalities in Italy with a high per capita income. I know about a nearby town, Pavia, where there exists such a statute.

On this Monday, people shop for fresh produce from vendors at Piazza delle Erbe's small farmers market, where I buy a few pieces of fruit for later, and then do a little browsing in the shops.

Walking around Verona some more, I check out the menus at different restaurants. When I find one that has gnocchi, I make a mental note to return after seven thirty for dinner. My friend Joe, the wine expert and foodie whom I met on the train to Florence, told me that Verona is the place to try gnocchi, so I will be a little more adventurous with my meal choice tonight.

Instead of eating dinner at Piazza delle Erbe, I discover another charming place away from the crowds. *Ristorante S. Eufemia* is tucked away in an alley closer to the river. Considering the number of tables outside as well as inside, this restaurant is much larger than I first thought. The atmosphere outside is to my liking and I order the gnocchi in a gorgonzola cheese sauce, which is delicious. I confess that I have never tried gnocchi before, thinking I would not like it because it is prepared with potatoes. What have I been missing all this time, I think. How fortunate that an acquaintance in Florida told me to try the gnocchi in Italy, and then never have it again except when I return here. I guess first sampling it in Italy is a good idea since it turns out to be so tasty. I may even order it again before I leave for home.

This morning I awaken on my third day in Verona and shortly afterward I am on the train to Bergamo. I arrive at 10:00AM and take a bus from the train station up the hill to *Bergamo Alta*, the upper part and historic center of Bergamo. My friend, Olga, is enthusiastic about my visit to Bergamo, "You will enjoy it." This town is built on a hill like many others in Italy, but by now the steps and inclines don't bother me anymore. I love walking around and looking for the old fortress, *La Rocca* up high on a hill. From this vantage point I am treated to a panoramic view of the city as well as a quiet atmosphere in the park surrounding the tower.

The little streets and shops confirm Olga's descriptions and *Piazza Vecchio* is a wonderful spot to people watch. Although I mingle with other tourists here, Bergamo Alta is not very crowded. The pleasant smells of freshly baked pastries fill every street, and flowers abound. I love the flowerboxes in Italy. I see pots of flowers or flowerboxes with colorful blooms at nearly every house. The oldest grey structure ends up having its own character with a flowerbox full of color. These scenes fascinate me; I want to capture the image of them with my camera wherever I go in Italy. This is another instance of how the Italian people make the most of nature around them and make everything look beautiful.

Two funiculars operate here in Bergamo; I am prepared to take one up to the highest point to see *Castello San Vigilio*, but like most shops in Italy, even the funicular does not run between one and three. I always forget about this afternoon closing of almost every business and, therefore, I am repeatedly disappointed, to say the least. I notice that the prices in the Bergamo shops are lower than in Verona, and I see laundry hanging out once again on balconies and beneath windows.

After a while I feel a little tired and need a rest from walking, so I have lunch, a pomodoro and mozzarella bruschetta, toasted bread with tomato and fresh mozzarella cheese, at *Ristorante Campanello.* Olga, thank you for telling me about this wonderful place. I do indeed like it.

On the train ride back to Verona, I observe row after row of grape vines, and farmers are out cutting their fields of grain. The train offers a good option for seeing a lot of the area.

Once in Verona, I head to beautiful Piazza delle Erbe for my last evening here. I choose to eat dinner at the outdoor restaurant, *Ai Lamberti*. Tomorrow I will be in Milan.

The early train *to Milano Centrale* has me there by 9:30AM. I am supposed to meet my friend Angela at the ticket room. This train station is huge. We are wise to have an agreed meeting spot. I am excited to see her after more than a year. She isn't here yet and I am looking around for her. After about ten minutes I spot her at the other end of the ticket room. Angela is so petite and always looks like the picture of fashion with a scarf perfectly tied and positioned around her neck.

After hugging each other we immediately get on the *Metro*, subway, to see some of Milano. She now works in *Arenzano*, a town on the Ligurian coast. Because of her former job in Milan, she knows the city well, so she is my tour guide for my first time here. We converse in English and in Italian. Milan is not exactly a major tourist destination when you compare it to Rome, Florence, or Venice. This big city is more business-oriented. It certainly has its attractions, though, and today is the day to see them.

Coming up the steps of the Metro at the *Duomo* stop, I cannot believe the sight in front of me. This huge Gothic cathedral is right here, larger than life, , and seeing it for the first time almost takes my breath away!

I always thought the Duomo in Florence was an incredible sight, but I think this one is even more spectacular. It can hold 40,000 people and is one of the largest cathedrals in the world. Its construction took over 500 years, with renovations always continuing. It truly is an amazing sight.

The only interruption that takes away from this awesome experience is the run-in I end up having with a street vendor who is not Italian. I am caught off guard. Having been in small towns the past two weeks, I am not expecting the pushiness from this African man selling some type of beads. After saying no twice, on the third try I become impatient with him and raise my voice to get rid of him once and for all. Immediately he tells Angela in Italian that I am prejudiced and she tries her best to de-escalate the situation, later telling me that it is best to just ignore these roving street vendors. Many immigrants from Morocco and Tunisia have come into Italy and are causing a huge problem for the Italians. In the future I will be more aware, especially in the big cities.

Across the street from the Duomo is the beautiful *Galleria Vittorio Emanuele II*, and as we are walking toward it, Angela says, "At Christmas, this shopping area is lit up and presents a beautiful scene. The arcade and indoor mall contain many different types of shops, and offer a pleasant place to walk and browse."

On the floor of the Galleria's center is a painting of an ox, with a hole in the pavement where his genitals should be. The hole was created from people stepping in this area and twirling around, believing that this will bring good luck. Of course, at Angela's urging, I have to try it too, and she has to take a picture of me doing it.

We walk over to *Teatro alla Scala*, the famous opera venue La Scala, which is over 200 years old. How could any of us forget that scene from *Moonstruck* when Cher and Nicholas Cage meet each other at the Metropolitan opera in New York City? I have yet to see an opera but feel something special just being here and wishing that someday I can get tickets to attend an opera performance in Italy.

We have a bite to eat on the top floor at *La Rinascente*, the very fashionable but expensive department store. The views of the Duomo from here are wonderful, as is the fresh lunch of panini.

More browsing after our break. A friend of Angela's meets up with us as we continue on to *Castello Sforzesco* by way of the Metro. This castle was built in the 1300s and is impressive.

Walking around on this hot day is tiring, so the nearby *Parco Sempione*, a large city park, is a welcome prospect for us. We need a respite in the shade. Today's temperature of eighty-two degrees does not seem to be too hot, but we are feeling it.

When Angela has to go home to Arenzano, we take the Metro back to the station and say our goodbyes. "Grazie Angela. Thank you for taking two trains to Milan to see me."

Hugging each other, we know this will not be the last time we meet. *"Margie, tu sei la mia buona amica. Ciao."* You are my good friend, Margie.

I feel happy.

Then I walk the short distance back to *Hotel Berna*, where I am staying. I spend the evening in the hotel lobby with some Canadians, Americans, New Zealanders, and some travelers from England. All of us are speaking English and comparing notes as to our various itineraries. I don't need any dinner as we are partaking of the aperitivo with drinks and various appetizers provided by Massimiliano at the bar. It is a great way to unwind after a tiring day in the city. Milano reminds me a little of New York, and I love it.

Tomorrow morning I will meet my brother and sister-in-law at *Malpensa* airport, as they arrive from the States. We will travel together for the next two and a half weeks. Now I am really excited and ready to have some company. I recall that the very first time I came to Italy was with both of them. They are a lot of fun.

I am up early and walk to the area next to the train station, where there is the stop for the Malpensa Shuttle bus to the airport. I purchase tickets from the driver and get on the bus, happy for once not to have a piece of luggage with me. It takes a little over an hour to reach the airport so I enjoy the ride on the comfortable touring bus.

It's Friday the 13th and I am at the airport waiting for Rick and Monica to emerge from the customs area. Pretty soon I see them proceed through the doors and I am thrilled they are here. After more than four weeks traveling solo, I am really happy to have some of my family here to share the next two and a half weeks. After hugs and smiles, we exit the airport and head toward the bus stop and ride the Malpensa Shuttle back to the center of Milan.

"You must be hungry and tired," I say. "Let's check you into our hotel. Then we'll go across the street for lunch."

"Great! We'll order pasta pomodoro," Monica says and grins." See where this comes from?

Rick yawns. "We both are feeling the jet lag. I want to go to sleep."

"We'll have lunch," Monica says, "and then, I think, we'll take a nap for a couple of hours."

"And I can use the time to catch up on my writing," I say.

In the early evening we take advantage of Hotel Berna's great aperitivo in the bar, and certainly have no need for any more food after bruschetta, pizza, and various vegetable dishes, along with a glass of *Chianti*. The friendly bar manager, Massimiliano, who likes to be called Max, makes it a fun event, and we are quite content. Tomorrow will be a full day of sightseeing and walking in Milan.

Following a delicious breakfast at the hotel I guide Rick and Monica on their first look at Milan. We won't be riding the Metro since Rick always wants to get as much exercise as possible, which means walking all day. So there is no question that the three of us will catch plenty of exercise today.

The weather is conducive to being outside; it is cloudy and not as hot as yesterday. The forecast calls for rain, though.

By ten o'clock we are already on the streets of Milan, walking down *Corso Buenos Aires*, which eventually becomes *Corso Vittorio Emanuele II*. As we arrive at Piazza del Duomo, the sight of the Duomo is not as dramatic for me as the first time, coming out of the Metro steps. But it still is pretty amazing.

We want to see the interior of the Duomo; I am surprised that the line in front of the entrance is short and that there is no charge. Inside, I cannot get over how huge the cathedral is. The ceiling is very high and every structure is just big, not elaborate or fancy like in some other churches and cathedrals, still very imposing. Afterward we go to the Galleria and take photos but skip stepping on the bull's genitals.

"Now I'll take you to the designer fashion street of *Monte Napoleone*," I say.

We check out the fashions and prices in the range of €800 for a pair of men's shoes and €500 for a sweater. A woman's pantsuit is on display for €3700. Incredible. Although we are keeping our eyes open, we do not spot any celebrities.

By the time we are ready for lunch, we remember that Italian restaurants close by two thirty, so we walk to an *alimentaria,* food store, and pick up some fruit, focaccia, salami, and cheese. On the way back to our hotel, we notice a bar, actually an English pub, just around the corner from our lodging. Since it is open and serving customers, we have lunch there anyway. We figure we can save the other food we bought for later.

After a quick rest in our hotel and a Skype call home, we go to Mass at a small church nearby, and then spend the early evening in the bar with Max for our last night in Milan. We need to pack and go to bed early, since we plan to leave the hotel just after seven in the morning to take the train to *Levanto* and the *CinqueTerre*.

Cinque Terre and Sicily

We are lucky to reach the train to Levanto during a rain-free spell. But we expect a day of rain and the sky looks as though the prediction might hold true. Luck happens to stay with us because when we arrive in Levanto, our base for two days in the Cinque Terre, there is no rain, and we walk the fifteen-minute downhill, though rugged, road to our hotel and check in.

"The weather seems to be cooperating" Rick says, "I think we can go to *Monterosso* and hike those trails."

When we come up the steps from the train station there, we are met with a sunny sky and the beautiful, blue Ligurian Sea.

How fortunate for us to find a wonderful little outside restaurant to have lunch right next to the ocean. Can you guess what we are ordering? Again, life doesn't get much better than this. I am so glad to have Rick and Monica here.

During our meal, though, the sky is grey and a little rain is starting, so we decide to take the train to *Riomaggiore*, as the sky looks sunny in that direction. It turns out to be a good decision, because when we arrive, the sun is shining, so we wander the easy route on *via dell' Amore* to *Manarola*, enjoying the scenic views of the cliffs and the rocks down to the ocean.

Via dell'Amore is the easiest of the hikes, only two kilometers along the seaside, and it offers beautiful views. All along the walk are padlocks with lovers' names and initials as symbols of their eternal love for each other. It's a fun hike to Manarola.

Manarola is a lovely village. We saunter through the streets, enjoy the people and the shops, and take a lot of photos. The streets are steep and consist of staircases and inclined walkways winding and twisting around the town.

Eventually we start to hike the second section on the Cinque Terre trail from Manarola to *Corniglia,* but after fifteen or twenty minutes the path is blocked. To our surprise we discover that it is actually closed; signs indicate that it is unsafe to proceed. Once we look around, we can see where an earlier rockslide now blocks the path. Who knows when this happened, but it would be nice if a sign were posted before we started this section to alert us that the remainder of the trail is closed.

So, after turning around, we return to Manarola and take the train back to Levanto. By now our feet need a rest anyway, since tomorrow we will be doing the more strenuous sections from *Monterosso al Mare* to *Vernazza* and then to Corniglia.

We are staying at the small family-run seventeen-room *Hotel Primavera.* Carlo is the friendly owner. When we tell him about our day and about the trail being closed, he says, "*Chiuso per un anno.*" It has been closed for a year. Interesting, and there still are no signs indicating the closure until the actual rockslide area. This lack of information is another example of experiences the

U.S. tourist may encounter in Italy. Like temporarily closed businesses in the mid afternoon, these inconveniences can be frustrating, but also are part of what makes these small villages so charming.

After we have a light dinner at a café near the hotel, we wander around the town till we come to the beach. It is still light out; the ocean is beautiful with the big waves crashing against the rocky cliffs that come down to the shore. Off to the right side, we watch quite a few surfers in wetsuits riding the waves. I am so surprised because I did not realize that Levanto is one of the top surfing spots in Italy. In fact, Carlo tells us later that in November of 2011 Levanto will be hosting the World Longboard Surfing Championships.

Sometimes life in Italy is a lot more difficult than I am used to in the States. An instance of this situation is the inconvenience I run into at an Italian bank. For the most part I use Bancomats to withdraw money in euros while traveling, but today I enter a bank in Levanto to change two €50 notes for smaller denominations. What I expect to be a simple process is a major production Italian style.

To enter the bank I have to stand in front of a circular holding area with room for one person, then an automatic door opens, allowing me to stand inside. I have visions of the old *Star Trek* series and am sort of waiting to hear a voice say, "Beam me up, Scotty." Anyway, once I am inside, the door closes and a door on the opposite side opens and now I am in the bank.

No clients are in this bank, and there are no teller windows, just a few desks with bank personnel sitting behind them. I stand near one of the desks until the man behind the desk indicates for me to come forward. When I show him the two €50 notes and ask for *resto*, change, I have to mention the name of the denominations for him to understand what I need. I expect him to take the €100 and hand me the equivalent in small bills, but this is Italy and nothing can be that simple.

The Italian gentleman types on his computer for at least three minutes without speaking to me, and then has to ask a colleague for help. After quite some time he deposits the two €50 notes into a machine, smaller bills come out, which he hands to me. I thank him and exit the bank through the same compartment door system. The whole process takes ten minutes although it feels like half an hour to me.

If I were home in the U.S., I could simply obtain change at any store or gas station when making a purchase. In Italy, whenever I try that at a coffee bar, in a train station, or a small shop, it does not work. Frequently the people who work at these places do not have much cash available and cannot make change even when I make purchases. I now know that it is really best to keep a supply of coins and small denomination euro notes handy.

A visit to the Cinque Terre makes my long-time wish come true. Photos, videos, and Rick Steves's talk about the five villages built into the cliffs in northern Italy, put the region known as Liguria on my itinerary. I do not mind the detour on my extended trip.

Although there is a regional train that runs along the coast connecting one village to another, the beauty, charm, and sense of adventure of the Cinque Terre lies in hiking along the trail from one village to the next village.

Travel books advise that the two longest sections of the trail are challenging and could be dangerous, but I tell myself that we are prepared for the next leg of our journey. The numbers of people with walking sticks, hiking boots, and backpacks should have been my first clue that this really is a trek for serious hikers, which the Germans are. They know what to expect and are the ones with the appropriate hiking gear. Still nothing can dampen my spirits of hiking this trail.

"I think I will stay home and take the day off," Monica says.

So it is my brother and me, and as an unplanned warm-up, we take the long way around to the train station (In other words, we get lost). We start on the hardest hike from Monterosso to Vernazza, supposedly a ninety-minute hike. At first it does not seem too hard but as time moves forward, it is definitely living up to the warnings of being very challenging, steep, and at some points dangerous.

There are many points on this trail, a former goat path, where my brother has to wait for me to catch up. I definitely regret not being in better shape for this ordeal. I have to add that my brother, Rick, is in excellent shape. He cycles between forty and sixty miles almost every day after walking at least five miles. It is not so much the inclines but the numerous staircases in both directions on uneven pieces of rock that make this climb challenging.

Rick is a good sport and is very patient with me, always cautioning me to be careful. My shoes are loose, so they are not the greatest footwear for this trail. Athletic shoes would be much better but it is too late now. Who else wears black leather Easy Spirits on hikes?

The redeeming factor is that all the way along the trail, the scenery is overwhelming. We are either along the sea or in a shaded forest area. On this four-kilometer section alone, we hike from sea level to the highest point of 720 feet, but since the trail leads up and down multiple times, the ascent actually measures more than 1500 feet, and the same for the descent, I later learn.

At one point near the end of this section, all of a sudden below us appears the most breathtaking view of the colorful village of Vernazza! How gorgeous it looks with its pastel-colored houses sitting almost on top of one another on a cliff, and a beautiful, green-colored ocean at Vernazza's shore. Wow, every pain is worth this one scene!

After three hours of hiking we finally arrive at Vernazza, and my feet are feeling it. I am so looking forward to sitting down for lunch. The town is very picturesque and charming. I wish

Monica could be with Rick and me, but I think she was wise to give her feet a rest.

We have a wonderful lunch at an outdoor restaurant with a view of the ocean. I am already trying to mentally prepare myself for the next section of the hike when Rick says, "Listen, Margie, I would not be disappointed if you do not want to hike anymore."

"Really?" It does not take more than a second or two for me to decide that I am content to walk around Vernazza instead. It's not like I am an avid hiker and have something to prove to anyone. I am enjoying the moment and loving my brother for giving me an out.

I have no way of knowing it now, but in less than six months the town of Vernazza will be devastated from a terrible mudslide and flood. Monterosso will also be damaged heavily but not as badly as Vernazza. I think we are more affected by news of disasters when we are familiar with the places that are devastated. I am happy to already report the two towns' recovery after much hard work and outside support.

After lunch we take the train to the hilltop town of Corniglia, which is the smallest of the five villages and the only one with no shoreline. Corniglia has a population of just over 200 people. From its train station there are only two options to reach the hilltop village.

One option is a shuttle bus that drives up to Corniglia and the other one is walking the 382 steps up to the top. Obviously we choose the bus but we have to wait for it because it is timed with the trains. Once we arrive at Corniglia, we check it out for a while and then take the bus back down the hill to catch the train back to Levanto. I really like the Cinque Terre. The entire area is just beautiful, including Levanto, which is a perfect place to use as our base.

It is okay that I returned without hiking the second part of the trail.

We meet Monica for dinner and afterward walk around Levanto, stopping for a gelato. I am glad to locate a laundry here. While Rick and Monica wait outside for me I do a couple of loads of wash. During the wash cycle, however, we leave for half an hour and discover an orthopedic shoe shop across the park. My feet are killing me, particularly my right foot. The shoes I wore for the hiking definitely were not good. And the Italian sneakers from the Siena shoe store are not that supportive either. At this point I don't care much about foot fashion as long as my feet don't hurt. I hope to find some athletic shoes here.

I am in luck because they have a pair of Dr. Scholl's athletic shoes that fit me and feel right. The cost doesn't matter to me. So I make the purchase. Afterward we return to the laundromat to deposit my clothes into the dryer, browse around some more, and, eventually, retrieve my clean, dry clothes. We return to our hotel to unwind and plan ahead.

After a good night's sleep I am ready for a busy travel day with six different modes of transportation, including walking, taxi, train, bus, plane, and rental car. The train ride takes three hours to Milano, followed by an hour on the bus to Malpensa airport, and followed by a flight of an hour and forty minutes to *Palermo*, Sicily, our destination for the next six days.

On the way to the airport I review our Palermo hotel reservations and suddenly discover a requirement to check in by 1:00PM or make other arrangements. Of course by this time it is already past one, so it is a little bit of added stress, as I try to think of a solution.

Eventually I am able to make contact with the hotel by phone. The woman acknowledges that she will wait for another call from us and will open the hotel in the evening when we arrive. Apparently it is a twenty-room hotel with a reception desk that operates on limited hours. From now on I must pay closer attention to these details when I make reservations.

This frustrating situation is just the start of a very stressful day. Although the rental car process proceeds smoothly, we end up driving around Palermo for three hours in the dark, getting lost, and having no clue how to find the right roads. It does not help that none of them are marked or that there are numerous roundabouts and a lot of traffic. The exit we are told to take ends up somewhere other than where we need to go. We have a GPS with an Italian instruction booklet in the car, so it is basically useless. My knowledge of Italian is not good enough to read an instruction booklet on operating something technical.

To say we are all frazzled is an understatement: and add that to being tired after traveling all day. This search for our hotel is not the best part of our trip. We decide to stop and ask someone for directions at the train station and with luck I find a friendly person who is happy to help us. He actually walks outside with me to the car where Rick and Monica are waiting. He then directs us to where we need to go. Finally we locate the hotel and check in at 10:30PM. The woman at the hotel must have the patience of Job because she greets us with a smile and three bottles of water. She even provides a cornetto for each of us, correctly assuming that we may be hungry. We are definitely hungry but we are too tired to go anywhere in search of something to eat. We just want to get some sleep, so her generosity is greatly appreciated. Our rooms here are huge, very comfortable, and quiet. So far our view of Palermo is not too positive. In the morning we will hopefully be able to see a brighter side to this historic city and capital of Sicily. Vediamo.

After a good night's sleep, Rick, Monica, and I want to walk around the center of Palermo for at least a few hours and enjoy what we can in the light of day. Palermo actually is lovely, and I am glad we have even a little time to see parts of it during the day when we are rested. I love talking with the people and there are plenty of them outside, selling everything from food to clothes. I need some white socks to wear with the Dr. Scholl's I bought in Levanto and this is a perfect spot to buy a pair. Purchasing the socks is such a pleasant experience as the Palermo people are happy to sell their merchandise, and they are not pushy either.

My favorite encounter today is with a shoemaker named *Gino Conciauro*. Standing outside his shop on *via Monteleone* he looks very comfortable in his navy-blue sweater vest and blue jeans. "*Buon giorno, Signore. Permesso di guardare?*" I ask. Good morning, sir. Permission to watch? Signor Conciauro allows us to go inside to observe the other shoemaker as he cuts the black leather to make a pair of men's shoes by hand. Outside the shop, the men's shoes are lined up on racks. The prices are incredibly reasonable for a pair of hand-made Sicilian leather shoes.

I know that I would never see this process of shoes crafted by hand in the U.S. and it is just one of those special moments for me. Gino proudly shows us a wall of postcards from all over the world and he is particularly proud of the ones from New York. He seems to be elated that we stopped by his shop, and he even poses for a photo, making me promise that I will send him a copy.

Life seems simpler here in Sicily and everything seems to cost a little less too. The people are especially happy to talk to someone who is from America. When I start to converse with one of the vendors at the outdoor market, I say, "*Buon giorno, Signora. Io sono Americana. Mia nonna e mio nonno sono nati in Sicilia.*" Good morning, Ma'am. I am American. My grandmother and my grandfather were born in Sicily. When they understand that our grandparents were born in Sicily and came to America from the port of Palermo, the local citizens are even more pleased. None of those who talk with me have ever been to the U.S., but invariably someone has a cousin who went to America, and they are excited to share this information with me. I wish there were more time to spend in Palermo and talk with the people here, but we decide to drive to *Cefalù* and enjoy some beach time.

The drive to Cefalù is scenic and does not take very long. Timing could not be any better after our stressful day yesterday. Our hotel is in a perfect location just opposite a beautiful beach, and, in fact, the view from the balcony of the room is the beach. A day of relaxation here is perfect with weather made to order. The seascape in Cefalù is impressive with homes that are built right down to the water. Towering high above them is this giant rocky crag known as *la Rocca*, the Rock. At 888 feet high, this landmark of Cefalù contains the ruins of an ancient castle and fossils.

We spend the afternoon on the crescent-shaped beach, where the sand is clean and the water of the Tyrrhenian Sea is turquoise blue. I wish I could stay here forever. After a couple of hours though, it is time to walk to the historic part of town and do a little exploring. *Corso Ruggero* is the main drag and there are no cars allowed, so people are walking in the street, which is lined with shops and palazzi. This place has the ambience of a small Sicilian town, inviting me to get lost in its little side alleys. Instead, Rick, Monica and I keep walking on the main street until it runs into *Piazza del Duomo,* which seems to be the center of the historic district. Palm trees line the sidewalks, a perfect venue for people watching.

At the edge of the piazza is the Duomo, a magnificent thirteenth-century cathedral built in the Norman-Romanesque style of architecture. Its tall twin spires loom high above all else and contribute to the skyline of Cefalù. Some Sicilian men sit on steps as they relax and converse with each other. The air feels hot today, so these men are wise not to exert themselves in the heat.

As we walk back toward our hotel, we stop for dinner at a small casual place. Afterward Monica and I walk to a gelato shop while Rick finds an internet café. I watch with interest as some teenagers eat their gelato in a very unique way. They make an ice cream sandwich out of a hamburger bun and chocolate gelato. Very interesting. I do not know about this phenomenon now but later learn that this is a favorite in Sicily; the bun is not a hamburger bun but a sweet roll known as a *brioche.*

Once I am back in my hotel, I catch a glimpse of what looks like a developing spectacular sunset. I grab my camera, run down the steps and out the door, and cross the street to the beach. The sky looks awesome and I am in time for one of the most magnificent sunsets on the water since I arrived in Italy last month. This is the perfect end to a fantastic day in Sicily, and one that I will always be able to remember, thanks to the magic of digital photography.

On the way to *Catania* we make a stop in *Cesarò*, the small village where my maternal grandparents were born. This is also Angela's home town. Her parents still reside here, so we plan to stop and see them. On the road to Cesarò, we drive past the town of *San Fratello* and through the *Nebrodi Forest*, where the foliage is a lush green color. As we approach Cesarò, much to our surprise, we encounter a group of cows wearing bells. They are strolling slowly down the middle of the same road on which we are driving. How hilarious to see this and so unlike a typical day at home in America, at least in Florida. We are in the Sicilian countryside, though, and cows on the road are probably a common occurrence.

Rick and I are out of the car, taking photos and videotaping the event to preserve it forever, while we are laughing. This is definitely one of the high points of the day, as the scene seems so surreal. "In 2007," I say, "during our first visit to Cesarò, we saw sheep in the middle of the road."

"I remember," Rick says. "I have pictures of that too."

Driving in Cesarò is certainly challenging. The old streets were made for pedestrians and possibly bicycles and small cars. Although we had ordered a medium-size car, we have a full-size Peugeot that absolutely does not navigate well in these streets. "Watch it, Rick!" Monica screams. "Don't drive down that staircase." At other times Rick realizes that we are driving the wrong way on a one-way street. With a little help from various friendly neighbors, we finally locate the house of *Maria Cillipollo* and *Antonino Savoca*, the mother and father of Angela. Although the couple are married, a woman retains her maiden name in Italy; hence the separate names. Maria is thrilled to see us!

"*Buon giorno, Signora Maria. Come sta?*" Good morning Ms. Maria. How are you? We take turns hugging this short smiling woman and then address her husband, since this is our first time meeting him. "*Questo è tuo marito? Piacere, Signor Savoca.*" This is your husband? Pleased to meet you, Mr. Savoca. Both Angela's father and mother have the bluest of eyes, unlike our grandparents, whose eyes were brown. Maria and Antonino speak only Sicilian, so the communication is a challenge but we seem to manage fine. Our visit together is pleasant, although short. We politely decline their repeated offers to feed us, since we still have to drive to Catania. Rick retrieves his hat from Signor Savoca. "*Grazie*," he says and smiles to thank him for safely keeping it for the past four years. After taking a few photos, we say our goodbyes.

Since Cesarò is such a small town, there are no real stores selling food items. To Monica's delight, she spots a familiar vehicle. "Look," she says, "that's the same fruit and vegetable truck that we saw during our first visit here."

But the driver is not selling produce now. He is driving the truck out of the town, so we are just a little too late to be able to buy anything from him. After we leave Angela's parents' home the few shops in town are closed too.

It is now one thirty and we grab a quick lunch at the only bar that is open, *Bar Saraniti*. Unfortunately this is one of the rare times I have to admit that the food is not very good. In hindsight, maybe we should have eaten at the house of Angela's parents.

I am disappointed that the municipio, the official records office, is closed, as I had hoped to look up some documents while here. To my regret, the church where my grandparents were most likely baptized is also closed. Again, it is the afternoon, and everything closes for a few hours. When will I remember that?

Cesarò looks probably much like it did when my grandparents lived here, as everything appears to be very old. The door frames fascinate me, since I love the look of the ancient doorways, especially in the oldest parts of town. Some of the doors are very short, reflecting the size of the Italian people, not generally known for their stature. As dilapidated as some of these doorways are, they have character, and I see a photo opportunity every time. I wish we had more time as life moves slowly here, but we have to leave if we want to make it to Catania before evening.

It feels like a major accomplishment to make it out of the village without damaging the car or people's property. And now we are on our way to Catania.

Visits with Teresa and Antonella

Monica especially likes cities and wants to go to Catania, the second-largest city in Sicily. Situated on the eastern coast of the island, it is not too far from *Taormina*, where Angela's sister, Teresa, lives. So this time we are going to stay in the center of the city and do some exploring. With the GPS finally programmed in English, thanks to instructions in the Peugeot manual, we have no problems finding our hotel in downtown Catania. Once checked into our rooms, we discover to our delight that we each have great views of Mt. Etna from our hotel windows. After a short search we find a place for dinner, which turns out to be one of the best meals of our trip.

Al Carpaccio is not far from our hotel; when we arrive, a sign informs us to ring a bell, and soon afterward the owner opens the door and welcomes us inside. Since it is only seven fifteen, early by Italian dinner standards, we are the only ones here and are treated like VIPs. After taking our orders the owner disappears into the kitchen. I think he is actually the one cooking the food. No one else appears to be working here. He also brings us our drinks and our meals. As expected, he speaks to us in Italian and I love it.

We relish the warm homemade pieces of focaccia he brings to the table instead of the usual basket of bread. All of us decide on pasta which he explains is freshly made, so we order three different dishes, *pappardelle, gnocchi,* and *penne rigate.* Pappardelle is similar to fettuccini, although the flat noodles are much wider. Gnocchi is pasta made with potatoes and looks like tiny dumplings. Penne rigate is thin-tubed, ridged pasta with diagonally cut ends. The individual insalata is big enough for two or three people; everything is just perfect. After dinner we walk a little more, and then it's back to the hotel to get a good night's rest.

Catania has its seedy areas but today we are out for some sightseeing in the touristy parts of town. This large Sicilian city has some marvelous attractions and today is the perfect sunny day for walking around and exploring the best things there are to see in Catania.

Corso Italia and *Corso Etna* are the main drags here, and they provide a lot of great photo ops. Catania has a population of almost 300,000. It is an old city with its origin dating back to the years BC. The city of Catania has been almost decimated on several occasions, with a lot of the destruction happening in the seventeenth century. After a huge eruption from neighboring Mt. Etna most of Catania was covered in lava. Less than twenty-five years later, in 1693, a massive earthquake killed two-thirds of Catania's population.

The rebuilding of the historic part of Catania was in the baroque style of architecture. Many of these public buildings and monuments are in shades of grey since lava was used in the construction efforts. I find this interesting as I look at all the grey-colored monuments and large buildings around me. One of the more unusual monuments is the one called the Elephant Fountain, or *Fontana dell' Elefante*, located in the center of the main square, *Piazza del Duomo*. Made of black lava stone, the elephant has become a symbol for Catania. The outer marble facade of the Duomo, or Cathedral of Sant' Agata, is impressive, as are the *Antico Teatro*, the Ancient Theater, and *Parco Bellini*, Bellini Park.

After our day of sightseeing in Catania, we decide to return to the same restaurant to enjoy the good food and pleasant ambience of the previous evening. Again, we are not disappointed. Although I know better, I cannot pass up the dessert, Sicilian cannoli with pistachios from *Bronte*. Mmmmmm.

On this Saturday the GPS makes the drive to Teresa's house in Taormina so much easier. When we arrive at her address we recognize her standing outside to show us where to park. It feels so good to see her again.

"It's been four years since my first visit with you. I'm so happy to see you, Teresa," I say.

"*Si,*" Teresa enthusiastically responds. "And I am happy to see you," she says in English, proud of the fact that she now knows some English words.

Teresa speaks mostly Italian with us because her English course is very difficult, or as she describes, *molto difficile,* so my Italian is put to good use here, and Teresa has some practice in English.

As a teacher she is off today and opens her home to us for the next two days and nights. Teresa and Angela Savoca are sisters.

"Where did the time go," I say. I originally made contact with you about ten years ago while doing genealogy research on the internet." Now we are good friends even though I still cannot confirm a familial connection.

Their last name is the same as my mother's maiden name and their roots are in Cesarò, the birthplace of my maternal grandparents. "Your grandfather and uncles also emigrated to Cleveland, Ohio, the same as ours," Rick says. It seems like too much coincidence for us not to be family." Teresa agrees. So we consider each other family anyway.

Angela lives here in Taormina with Teresa when she is not working out of town. At this time, unfortunately, she is working in northern Italy, and Teresa is the only Savoca at home.

Today the three of us are going to *Caltagirone*, the Sicilian ceramics town, so Monica and I can buy some ceramics. Teresa's brother, *Calogero*, and her sister-in-law, Monica, live there, so Teresa makes arrangements for us to meet them. The plan is to drive to Catania and pick up Calogero, who works as a police officer there. Afterward we will go together to Caltagirone in two cars, because we are also delivering Angela's car to Calogero's house, since Angela is not using it while working in northern Italy.

Teresa tells us that Calogero and Monica have invited us to their home to share lunch with them, which Monica, an excellent cook, is preparing. I have tasted her cooking before and it is better than anything served in a restaurant. She has two complete kitchens in her home, an indication of how much she enjoys cooking. This meal is going to be a real treat!

At the police station we have to wait for Calogero for quite a while. Finally he walks toward our car. He is an attractive man and very friendly. After a brief introduction, he says with a smile,"*Vieni con me. Vi darò un tour e vi incontrare i miei colleghi.*" Come with me. I will give you a tour and you can meet my colleagues. More Italian practice for me.

Eventually we drive to their home in Caltagirone, where we meet his lovely wife, Monica, and their two children. Martina is fourteen, and Antonio will be twelve in two weeks.

Teresa phones Monica to tell her we will be delayed, which she seems to take it in stride as the wife of a police officer.

This whole family is wonderful and of course Monica has prepared a full-course meal. First we have sun-dried tomatoes, two types of olives, and mushrooms, all in olive oil. And, there is wine. The kids each have some along with the adults. Then Monica brings out her *pasta bolognese*, which is pasta served with a thick meat-based tomato sauce. She chooses hand-made *fusilli* as the pasta for this dish. This thin corkscrew-shaped pasta does not even resemble packaged fusilli. Every serving is delicious and the *pane* is just the best.

After we finish eating the appetizers and the pasta bolognese, Monica serves the *secondi piatti*, or second course, of chicken and potatoes. Rick, Monica, and I simply cannot eat any more, since the pasta serving was even too much at this point. I think Monica, the hostess, is disappointed, but we are not used to eating such a big meal in the middle of the day. This custom, that the largest meal is in the middle of the afternoon, is more common in Italy.

Following the main course are caffè and dolci, a variety of Sicilian sweets bought by Calogero at *Caffè Europa* in Catania. Calogero is trying his best to influence me to add some *Sambuca* to my caffè, but I politely decline. In Sicily this is a common practice but I am quite aware of the effect of this delicious anise-flavored liqueur. I think its alcohol content is close to fifty percent.

Martina has been taking English in school for eight years, as required in Italian schools, so she understands and speaks some. She helps translate for her parents during our conversation. The comfortable feeling I have amid this family is one of my favorite experiences since coming to Italy.

After Monica gives us a tour of their lovely home, Martina says goodbye to us as she leaves on her motor scooter to go to a dance. Although she is only fourteen, in Italy the law allows driving privileges on motor scooters at this age, but to drive a car you must be eighteen. The rest of the family, including Antonio, comes with us to the centro storico of Caltagirone.

Here is another example of the difference between Americans and Italians. Most twelve-year-old boys in America would not go with their family to visit ceramics shops. In Italy, though, many activities become events for the entire family. As a second-generation Italian-American I was raised in the convictions that family means everything. I really like this part of the Italian lifestyle.

This is not my first visit to Caltagirone but it is for my sister-in-law, Monica. I love this town and especially how life in it has some reference to ceramics. I am so impressed by that fact that I write articles about it. One of the coolest sights here is the giant staircase called *La Scalinetta*. There are 142 steps, and the risers of each step are made from hand painted majolica ceramic tiles.

They are unique in that no two tiles have the same design. Every summer a large festival is held to celebrate the feast of *San Giacomo,* Saint Joseph, the patron saint of Caltagirone. The steps are lit with thousands of tiny oil lamps, which create an awesome artistic display. People come from miles around to celebrate this big festival. I would love to see that sometime, but now, in May, the steps are decorated with flowers arranged to form a beautiful design. Naturally this turns into another photo op for all of us. I think Calogero and Monica are happy that we are enjoying their town.

Although there are hundreds of ceramic shops in this baroque town of almost 40,000 people, Monica and Calogero take us to the shop of *E. Boria,* a friend of Calogero's. Not only do we meet this artist who hand paints the ceramic pieces and see his work area where numerous ceramic pieces are in process, but anything we purchase is discounted for us, thanks to Calogero. My sister-in-law and I feel ecstatic at this good fortune.

After about an hour inside Boria's shop, I complete my purchases and now have some new additions to my ceramics collection. Obviously I will make another trip to the post office soon to ship these items home. By the end of the day we say our goodbyes to Monica, Calogero, and Antonio but not before we receive two lemons the size of grapefruit from their *giardino,* or garden. We drive back home to Teresa's in Taormina, and it's safe to say that we are tired and decide to call it a night. I learned a lot of Italian today.

This morning fa *tempo brutto*, the weather is ugly, cloudy, and raining. Eventually the rain slows down to a light drizzle on and off and we leave for the center of Taormina with umbrellas. I like this beautiful resort town on the blue Ionian Sea and could visit it again and again.

Although Teresa lives in Taormina, her house is in the lower section and not the touristy, historic area on the hill. Offering to drive us in her car, Teresa proves she is a pro at navigating these narrow, winding streets so commonly seen in Italy and with which we are now familiar. Taormina is a wonderful town to have fun just browsing around the little shops and taking photos while enjoying the panoramic views.

Later we take Teresa to lunch in *Giardini-Naxos*, the neighboring town along the beach. We have a favorite restaurant from our visit four years ago and want to return to *La Bussola*. To our delight we recognize the same two guys who were our waiters at our previous visit. The food again is fantastic and very reasonably priced. Sicily is definitely less expensive than most other cities in *Italia.*

After lunch we pick up Angelica, whom we know from an earlier visit. She is another friend of Teresa and Angela's. Angelica is a beautiful girl with a great smile and a tremendous personality. She speaks some English, so it's enjoyable to get together again with her. Teresa wants to take us to the seaside village of *Riposto* where the gelato is known to be some of the best, particularly the pistachio kind. Teresa explains that the pistachios are from the town of Bronte and simply are the best pistachios in all of Italy. Naturally I have to taste that flavor and cannot argue with Teresa. She is right: this gelato is terrific! And here I finally learn about the strange gelato in what looks like a hamburger bun. It is called *gelato in brioche*, and Teresa orders one. I realize now that these treats are very popular in Sicily.

As we savor our gelatos, we walk along the gorgeous harbor and take in the scene with all the boats docked there. I always love marinas; they make good backdrops for photos. Rick and Monica explore a little on their own near the harbor, and I practice some Italian in conversations in Italian and English with Angelica and Teresa. We have a great time. I love it.

Ultimately we must leave, so we say arrivederci after dropping off Angelica on the drive back to Teresa's. There we check some e-mail and make a few Skype calls, then go to bed. Tomorrow we leave early for *Colle d'Anchise*, which we have heard is an eight-to-ten hour drive from Taormina and includes a ferry ride across the strait of *Messina*.

Our destination today is Colle d'Anchise, the birthplace of Rick's and my paternal grandparents. After we say thank you and goodbye to Teresa, we leave for the port of Messina, where we catch the ferry, or *traghetto*, to *Villa san Giovanni*, the first town in *Reggio Calabria* on the mainland of Italy. The ferry ride lasts about twenty minutes and we enjoy the nice change of pace. The views of both Sicily and Reggio Calabria are interesting from the vantage point of a boat. The wind blowing against my face while I am standing on the deck feels wonderful this morning.

Driving through Reggio Calabria we notice that the area is very industrial with some new construction and a lot of tunnel work through the mountains. The mountainous region appears, however, to be mostly agricultural and is new to me.

When it is time for lunch, we stop in a small town called *Torano*, buy some gas, and ask the locals to suggest a place to eat. They direct us to the small *Ristorante Marchese Giose*, where we are lucky once again, to have the owner wait on us. Usually, where locals choose to eat the food it is definitely good. The prices here are low, affordable for Italian workers and great for us. The three of us order rigatoni pomodoro, yes, pasta pomodoro again, water, and bread for eighteen euros total. Included is a complimentary appetizer of *melanzane, egg*plant, *mortadella,* an Italian sausage the size of bologna and has small bits of pork lard, and bruschetta. This area of Italy is not touristy and I assume may be more affordable for the Italian to live.

We arrive in Colle d'Anchise close to five o'clock and the GPS does not recognize the address of the *agriturismo*, a simple rustic accommodation in Italy, where we have reservations. Once we arrive in the center of the village we ask the first person we see for directions. Just by luck, this young man is going fishing near the agriturismo and tells us to follow him in his car. Great, we have our own personal guide.

The little village looks nicer than I had expected. The surrounding hillsides are really scenic. When we arrive at the agriturismo, *La Piana dei Mulini*, we are met by a friendly young gentleman who shows us to our rooms. Once inside, the accommodations exceed my expectations by far. My room is completely new and very large. This is the first time I am staying in an agriturismo and so far I like it. I am surprised that a village this small might even have any accommodations, and it is only because my cousin *Antonella Baratta*, whom I will meet soon, recommends this place.

Everything about La Piano dei Mulini looks inviting, and we decide to have dinner at its restaurant later this evening. Besides, there really is nowhere else to go. Apparently this is a popular spot to eat because there are only seven rooms at the agriturismo, but the dining room is large and people keep coming in for dinner. The food is excellent and so is the ambience. It's just what we need after a long day of driving.

A town near here is called *Longano*, which is also my maiden name. As far as I know, no one from my family comes from that town. Rick, Monica, and I want to check it out. "So tomorrow morning let's just do that," I say.

Longano is an even smaller village than Colle d'Anchise.

After a wonderful breakfast in the dining room at our agriturismo we take a ride to the small town of Longano, which is approximately forty-five kilometers from Colle d'Anchise. We are very curious to see the village that has our name. Of course, on the way we have to stop and take pictures of each other standing next to the sign that says Longano. This is so not a tourist place and I am sure that anyone driving past must wonder what we are doing and why we are here.

The views of the mountains and countryside are phenomenal. Nature is clad in green, but in the distance we can see snow on a mountain top. The area is full of hills. Close to town, local people work in their gardens and hang out their laundry.

When we approach Longano, we find a beautiful small village nestled up in the hills. We park in the piazza and start to walk around. This comune of seven hundred people is very clean, with colorful flowers in bloom on doorsteps and balconies. The residents of Longano love their flowers as much as their neighbors do throughout Italy.

Some of the people in this town have features resembling my grandparents, although many have blue eyes, not brown. In the square, four older men are sitting on the church steps talking, and a fruit truck is parked here for anyone wanting to buy fresh produce. All three of us feel welcome and a connection with the people here because everyone is so friendly and happy. When we actually speak with the local people and tell them that we are Americans and that our name is Longano, they are so excited and can't stop talking to us. They treat us like celebrities, inviting us to come and stay for a month and telling us that they will cook a pigeon for us.

They are happy to say yes when we ask permission to take their photos, and several of them speak a little English and are eager to talk with us and translate for the others. One woman in particular is so excited to translate she keeps asking, "Do you want me to tell you what he just said?" She is so endearing and we find out she is eighty years old.

One man we meet is proud to inform us that he is the former chief of police. He seems to take on the role of the local host of Longano. Within a short time apparently everyone in the town knows about us, and they are talking about the Americans with the name of Longano. They cannot be any nicer. Eventually we know we have to leave and drive back to Colle d'Anchise, so we say goodbye and promise to return someday.

In Colle d'Anchise I am able to quickly locate this address: *10 Strada Campo di Maggio*, which is where *Angelo Longano*, my grandpa's father, died according to records I found doing genealogy research. The address is basically an old door and a small window on the side of a building with other small doors and small windows. I feel the connection to my family by just being here and walking the same streets that my grandparents must have walked when they lived here over a hundred years ago. Not many people are around. It is amazing to see a woman walking with a large scarf on her head, which is wrapped in such a way to hold a huge supply of greens. Another woman is sitting outside her home, cleaning fava beans.

I am supposed to meet Antonella, my fourth cousin, for the first time here. The first person I ask not only knows Antonella, but kindly calls her on her cell phone and then informs me that she is Antonella's mother! Her name is *Isabella* and she has a beautiful smile. Since she is the mother of Antonella she would be my third cousin, through marriage, because it would actually be Antonella's father that is my third cousin. It gets a little confusing.

Isabella also lives next door to the house where my grandmother was born. Later, however, when we go to find the address, I learn that there is no *14 Strada San Sisto*. Isabella tells me that at one point the numbers were changed so, unfortunately, nobody really knows which house would have belonged to my grandmother.

When Antonella arrives a few minutes later, I am thrilled to finally meet her in person after having communicated only by Facebook and Skype these past months. She is so friendly and is fluent in English, having lived in Canada as a young child. Rick, Monica, and I tour the little village of Colle d'Anchise with her and meet her grandmother who is eighty-nine years old. She is very kind and insists we enter her home. Within five minutes she starts preparing food for us. We feel really bad but we end up having to be firm in declining, and she is not happy, so I have to promise to return when I am back in Colle d'Anchise in early June.

We then walk to Antonella's home, which is not in the center of town but down the hill and more in the country. We spend a little time there. Although her home is small by American standards, it does not seem small; it is very comfortable and of course very clean. Pretty soon her husband, Michele (pronounced MEE- KAY-LAY), comes home for lunch. He works in a law office, I remember from Antonella's Facebook messages. Offices, like most businesses in Italy, close for a few hours in the afternoon. Michele and Antonella are very welcoming to us; it feels good being with a young family and seeing how they live.

Eventually we go back to our agriturismo and relax for a while. A few hours later, after her four-year-old son, *Gianluca,* comes home from school, and after his daily nap, Antonella picks me up in her car. Because Monica and Rick decide to rest at La Piano dei Mulini, only Antonella, Gianluca, and I go to the town center at *Campo Aperto,* its small park and playground. While Gianluca plays, I meet a few of Antonella's friends who are also young mothers with kids at the park. Antonella knows everyone there, having lived in the village since age four, and the village has only nine hundred residents. Life is simple here, and the people seem happy.

While we walk back from the park, I meet *Don Fredy*, the priest to whom I wrote in Italian regarding documents about my grandparents. He promises that I can look through the registers when I return in a few weeks. He will also give me what he has researched. Right now he is on his way to say Mass at one of the four churches here.

I meet the rest of Antonella's family, her sister *Carolina*, who manages the small *groceria*, grocery store. Later, at her mother's home, I meet her younger sister *Santina*, who is a hairdresser, working out of her house. She is also artistic, and sells some of her decoupage work, which is beautiful. All my local relatives are very friendly and I leave here with an invitation for dinner when I return by myself for three days in June.

Antonella drives me back to our agriturismo just in time for me to meet up with Rick and Monica for dinner. Again it looks as if someone is cooking just for us, since we are the only dinner guests in the restaurant tonight. This experience feels very personal, especially when our waiter brings me a cell phone with a call from *Signor Michele*, Mr. Michele, the owner of La Piano dei Mulini. He is inquiring if everything is *tutto bene*, all good. This is a great place to stay, and I am glad I will be returning next month.

On a side note: I lost my passport somewhere between Catania and here but, luckily, have a paper copy. Between phone calls to Teresa and speaking to Antonella, I am relieved to hear

Teresa say, "*Il passaporto è in hotel a Catania,*" Your passport is in the hotel in Catania. I vaguely remember leaving it in the safe at the *Excelsior Grand Hotel*. Antonella suggests that Teresa send it here to Antonella's address in Colle d'Anchise, where I can retrieve it when I return in early June.

The process seems questionable to me, knowing how much time many transactions take in Italy, but Teresa and Antonella convince me that my passport will arrive quickly. It seems that mail sent within Italy does not take that long.

Calogero, being a police officer in Catania, is to pick up my passport at the hotel and send it to Antonella's house. The process seems to be working because Angela calls me from northern Italy to tell me that Calogero has in fact received the passport and has already mailed it. So within twenty-four hours' time, thanks to my Sicilian friends, Teresa, Calogero, and Angela, along with my *cugina*, cousin, Antonella in Colle d'Anchise, the problem is solved!

Rome and the Amalfi Coast

Today we are leaving for Rome, but not before we make one more stop at the post office to mail the ceramics back home. Since this post office is in the tiny village of Colle d'Anchise, the process is much shorter and easier than in larger communities like Perugia. Only one person works here and nobody is waiting in line. After only fifteen minutes I am able to complete the process of mailing my package home. While I am at the post office, Antonella stops in to say goodbye one more time.

Rome is about a three-hour drive from Colle d'Anchise, and with Rick behind the wheel, we arrive without problems, drop off the rental car, and take a taxi to our hotel. I feel like I am reconnected to the rest of the world now that we have a phone signal and Wi-Fi again. Colle d'Anchise in the mountains is not the best spot to get a satellite signal and there simply is no Wi-Fi.

Rick, Monica, and I have a great lunch at *Ristorante Ambasciata Di Capri*, recommended by the front desk clerk at our hotel. Located close by, this place is off the beaten path, has authentic Italian food, and is frequented by the locals. When we arrive, *Mario*, the owner, is the one who shows us to our table, and he begins to sing almost immediately. We are happy with our pasta dishes of gnocchi, ravioli, and spaghetti. This is a great start to our four days in Rome together. After that I will travel solo again as Rick and Monica will head back home.

After a short rest in our hotel rooms, we walk to *Trastevere*, which is one of our favorite neighborhoods in Rome. I love this very trendy neighborhood; it has lots of little restaurants and small piazzas along the winding streets, much different from the heavy traffic of the touristy spots near the monuments. We spend most of the day wandering around and after checking out a few spots, we find another excellent spot for dinner on a side street near *Piazza San Cosimato*. The smells of fresh tomatoes and cheese are in the air as we approach the restaurant. Again we are eating outside, my favorite way to enjoy the food and the people in Italy.

Afterward we walk back to our hotel, and my feet are feeling it. I think we walked at least four miles each way, although my brother insists it was less. He is kicking my butt with the exercise, but my feet are killing me despite my Dr. Scholl's sneakers. Three more days of this regimen with my exercise-loving brother. Actually, I am really having a good time in Rome, much more than when traveling solo last month. Having Rick and Monica here with me is fun, and Rome is a lot less crowded than at my previous visit here a few weeks ago. Rome is always busy but rarely with crowds like those attending the beatification of Pope John Paul II.

Our hotel is in the *Prati* area, a perfect location, maybe even partly residential. We are doing a lot of walking every day, and did I mention that my brother is giving me a workout? I think his main agenda in Rome is to see how many miles he can walk in a day! Tomorrow the three of us are going to the Vatican together.

As agreed before our trip, our itinerary now includes our return to St. Peter's. We want to spend a lot of time inside, not at the Vatican Museum. While here at St. Peter's, I am very interested in seeing the special exhibit about John Paul II. While I browse its multi-media exhibits, I find myself becoming very emotional as I watch some of the videos and read some of the stories about him. The tomb of John Paul II is now also located in the main church, just to the left of Michelangelo's *Pieta*.

After about four or five hours inside, we are ready for lunch. We stop at one of the touristy restaurants just outside the Vatican and are disappointed. The service is poor and the food is nothing special. We should have known better, but when you are hungry you don't want to wait. The best food in Italy is always at smaller places on side streets and not in the main tourist area.

Later that day, as well as the next day, we do some of the touristy things and some not so touristy. Of course we go to the Spanish Steps, and spend more time in Trastevere, having dinner there one evening and some good pastry with apricot filling at *Bar Quadrani* on *Viale Trastevere*. This is one of our favorite spots from our trip here four years ago; we are thrilled that it is every bit as good today as the previous time.

This time our agenda definitely includes a return to another of our favorite spots, *Campo di Fiori*, Field of Flowers. Monica and I want to buy some great pizza at *Forno Campo di Fiori*, where we are able to watch the bread-making process from the door. We don't care that we have to walk around and eat it because there are no chairs inside.

While we are near the Campo de Fiori, it does not take us long to find that small store with the lady proprietor and the special biscotti that I love. I had promised her I would return with my brother and today is the day. She is thrilled to see me again, but I am not sure that she remembers Rick and Monica from four years ago, but they remember her. It feels good to know people so many miles away from home. Of course I buy a few more biscotti because I doubt that I will find these anywhere else. I would love to learn how to make this type of biscotti myself.

We also go to Borghese Park and then walk back over the *Ponte Cavour* bridge. It is hot in Rome but the good news is, there is no rain. On the walk back toward the Prati district, we feel hungry and discover a restaurant which looks interesting. *La Piccola Irpinia* is located very near our hotel, so we decide to give it a try. One of its features is an antipasto bar, which appeals to Monica and me. We enjoy our meal so much; I actually have some cold octopus salad with potatoes. Flavored with just the right amount of garlic and olive oil, the salad tastes fresh. I like it. This is a whole new food experience for me!

On our last day in Rome we take one of the Hop-on, Hop-off sightseeing buses and go to Santa Maria Maggiore, which is one of the most beautiful churches in Rome and one of Monica's favorites. The interior is awesome with its ornate marble columns, intricate mosaics, and decorated gold ceilings. I am glad we have time to visit here. We spend quite a bit of time exploring different parts of the church and taking photos of the elaborately decorated side altars, arches, confessionals, and doorways.

At one point we are definitely in need of some *stracciatella,* chocolate chip, gelato, so we head to Big Ben's in the *Esquilino* area, where we know from our previous trip together that the gelato is very good. Lingering here for a little time, we thoroughly enjoy one of Italy's best treats.

After we arrive back at the hotel we hug and express our sentiments, "It was so great being with you these past two weeks. See you soon at home."

Rick and Monica have to leave early in the morning.

Since I don't have to be on the train to Salerno until the afternoon, I am looking forward to meeting the oldest Savoca brother, *Salvatore,* at eight in the morning. He and his wife live just outside of Rome. We have plans to meet in the hotel lobby and spend time together until I leave on a fast train to Salerno.

When Salvatore and his wife, *Esin*, arrive in the morning at my hotel, we quickly get to know each other. The comfortable, quiet lobby is perfect for sitting and talking and sharing photos and stories. Both Salvatore and Esin are so friendly. Like me, Salvatore believes that our families must be related. He speaks several languages, including English. His wife, who is from Turkey, speaks Turkish and only a little Italian. She kindly invites me to their home today, but I still need to pack and leave on a train for Salerno in a few hours. I explain that there is not enough time but I really appreciate their hospitality. I hope that sometime in the future they will be able to come to America, and I can open my home to them.

Salvatore shares with me his dream of driving a motorcycle across America one day. Until then, we will share stories and photos on e-mail. After they leave, I finish packing, do some writing, and take a taxi to the Termini to catch the train to my next adventure.

Maiori is part of the beautiful *Amalfi Coast*, and lies just five kilometers past the town of Amalfi. The *SITA* bus ride from the train station in Salerno is a beautiful drive along the coastal road and cliffs, and probably the best €1.50 for my money since arriving in Italy almost eight weeks ago. Maiori has the longest beach of any of the towns along the Amalfi Coast. The residential part of the town is located up in the cliffs.

I am staying at a Franciscan monastery where friars actually live. The monastery sits right on the Amalfi Coast road along the sea. From my window I have the most beautiful view of the water. There is no air conditioning in my room, but the breeze off the sea makes it quite comfortable, even at the end of May. Maiori has a promenade all along the shore. On the boardwalk, wearing casual summer clothing, people amble past bars, gelaterias, and restaurants. Like them, I stroll up and down and familiarize myself with what I see here. As I mentioned, the road runs along the beach but is elevated. Opposite from the road are the many restaurants. After an early evening Mass at the church next to the monastery, I walk down the promenade to the interesting-looking *Ristorante La Vela*. I remember reading some recommendations about this restaurant and decide to try it for dinner.

I have a table with a view to die for. Compliments of the ristorante, I am served some seaweed bruschetta along with my dinner. The strands of seaweed prepared on a lightly toasted slice of bread, drizzled with olive oil and garlic, make a pleasant appetizer. Surprisingly, I like it! This is really of historical importance that now I have had both octopus and seaweed within days of each other!

The next morning at breakfast I discover that I am one of only two guests staying at the monastery. The *padre*, priest, and the woman who works here speak only Italian, as does the other guest, a signora from Rome. I have, thus, more opportunity to practice speaking the language. They seem pleased that I understand them and can converse in Italian.

I have no agenda for the day, and it just happens that the proprietor of the historic *Castle of San Nicola* is here this morning. The friendly woman employed at the monastery asks me to join her later when she drives this gentleman up to the castle at eleven. *"Grazie, sono molto felice di andare."* Thank you. I am very happy to go.

Against my earlier thoughts not to visit this castle, I now figure why not; then I can walk back for some exercise. My brother, Rick, will enjoy hearing about this, although he definitely would have declined the ride, opting to walk there and back.

Today the sun is shining and the air feels warm. I cannot believe I am staying along the Amalfi Coast with a view of the sea, and the sounds of the ocean waves at night. This alone would be an ideal vacation. Everyone in town is very friendly, greeting each other with a *buon giorno* or *buona sera,* good evening. A lot of the little shops look interesting. I will definitely have to check them out later. One is a sandal shop where the owner and his wife are sewing the sandals right in their shop.

As I sit in a beautiful courtyard at the monastery with a pergola shading me from above, I can smell the pleasant citrus aromas from the enormous lemons that are growing on the trees just above the pergola. Hanging hand-made ceramic lights adorn this peaceful setting where birds warble. Of course there is also a shrine to St. Francis. This terrace, a very tranquil spot, is a wonderful place to write. I am really glad I can spend five days here. After the busy agenda in Rome, this is a welcome repose.

At eleven I am ready to take the ride to the castle, but I don't know if I misunderstood: the woman is not going. Instead it is just me and *Crescenzo*, the seventy-three-year-old proprietor. I am game and figure this will be a new experience. Of course I realize too late that once Crescenzo drives his car as far as he can, there are over 300 steps to climb. I am not so sure my feet agree with my earlier consent (Rick will undoubtedly smile when he reads this!). After Cinque Terre, though, this isn't too bad, and Crescenzo climbs these steps every day. I must admit that he can go a lot faster than I and without taking any breaks. It is embarrassing that he is in better shape than I am.

Once we arrive at the castle, it turns out that I have my own, personalized tour with Crescenzo as guide, which is great. The castle is really mostly ruins at this point but still interesting. Crescenzo also takes care of necessary repairs at the castle, and has lemon trees and grape vines that he tends. It is obvious that he loves doing this work, and that he is eager to show me everything. The view from the top of the mountain is magnificent, not only of Maiori, but Crescenzo points out the town of *Ravello* with its famous landmarks, *Villa Rufalo*, and *Villa Cimbrone* on the next mountain high above Amalfi. It is interesting for me to see it from this vantage point, different from my earlier visit to the area.

After the tour I give Crescenzo twenty euros although he never asked for a fee. There is a jar with a sign that says donations, and for a personalized tour like this, I am sure that he will appreciate the twenty euros. I leave there with a freshly picked lemon and another memory of a kiss from an Italian man over the age of seventy! I am becoming accustomed to it. He is just a nice gentleman with a genuine smile.

Afterward I walk down the hill, stop at a mini-market, and buy some local provolone, salami, and fresh pane. Next, I go back to my room to change clothes for the beach. I think about how lucky I am to have a place to stay so near the sea. At the beach I find a spot close to the water and settle in to savor my home-made panini with aqua naturale. It feels so good to be in the warm sun on the Amalfi Coast. The beach is relaxing and the water temperature refreshing. The weather in late spring is more pleasurable than in October. I am thoroughly enjoying this!

The drive along Italy's Amalfi Coast is one of the most beautiful anywhere, if you are not the one driving. For a few euros you can take a blue SITA bus from one town to the other, and take in the incredible scenery along the Amalfi coast road from Maiori to *Minori* to Amalfi, to *Positano,* and other small villages in between. I hope these bus drivers are compensated well, because navigating a large bus on these steep winding roads, as well as the narrow streets within the towns, is a feat nothing short of a miracle. When two buses approach each other on a curve from opposite directions, there is no room for both. The bus coming uphill must back down the road to allow room for the bus coming down. They literally pass within inches of each other, as well as within inches of lampposts and other structures built along the road. It is an awesome if not scary experience.

Now that the temperatures are in the eighties every day, I do see many Italians wearing shorts, although most are young people. Moreover, I am in the south of Italy and notice the difference in how people are dressed. Perhaps it is partly due to the climate, but I see far less people wearing scarves and stiletto heels here. I also must amend my comments on the Italian bus drivers, as I am finding many to be more than helpful. Another thing I notice is that dogs seem to be welcome everywhere in Italy. I spot them on buses, trains, boats, in stores, restaurants, and on tours. One bar even has a bowl of water and a specific section marked "Dog Bar."

I have time in Italy to contemplate the Italian way of life and some observations in particular make an impression upon me. Each region in Italy is known for certain items either grown or produced in that area, such as olive oil, *vino*, wine, ceramics, and lemons, among others. The Italian people who live in those areas are proud of the items coming from their region; they are eager to share anything they can. It may be as simple as taking a lemon from their tree, scraping a little of its skin, and allowing me to smell its strong flavor.

They also seem very connected with the earth and appreciate whatever grows there naturally, using various herbs and plants to their benefit. Rather than taking these things for granted, the Italians have such a passion and appreciation for what grows around them; they tend to the soil to reap the most use out of it.

Today is the last day in May and the weather is quite warm. I am on the early bus to Amalfi, where I will be able to take a ferry to *Capri*. I purchase a ticket and wait a bit for the ferry, trying to locate myself on the deck, so I can shoot some photos. The views of the Amalfi Coast, and particularly Positano, are spectacular from the vantage point of the ferry. I see this part of the Amalfi Coast for the first time from a boat, not just from driving along the coastal road, so this is a real treat.

On approach to the island of Capri, the small ferry boat circles around various locations of the island, making for even more fantastic photo ops. This is almost like a boat tour of Capri instead of just transportation to the island. The water near Capri is an emerald green, as beautiful, I think, as I might ever imagine. I am surprised to see a mountainous Capri with cliffs, just like the mainland along the Amalfi Coast. But why would I expect a much flatter piece of land when in this part of Italy nothing is flat. This huge rock of an island seems imposing as the boat gets closer to the shore. The large *Faraglioni* rocks that rise up out of the sea in front of the island are awesome.

I give up my plan to visit the Blue Grotto and to wander about the town of Capri. After finding out that it would take two buses to reach the Blue Grotto and two to return, and a lot of time waiting around, I decide against it. Quite a few people tell me that the Blue Grotto is highly overrated, that three thousand tourists a day wait in line for a two- or three-minute visit. Instead I opt to go on a walking tour with *Vincenzo*, a tour guide who comes from *Sorrento*, knows the island of Capri well, and speaks fluent Italian and English. So for only twenty euros, Vincenzo promises to show a group of us all around the island of Capri, including the mountaintop town of *Anacapri* and the non-touristy areas I probably never would have seen otherwise. It is a good decision.

Even though I usually dislike tours, our group is small and Vincenzo allows for plenty of free time in both towns. In fact I manage to have a refreshing gelato in Capri on this hot day and also do a little shopping. One of my coworkers has a little girl named Capri. She would like me to bring her a snow globe from here. Not only do I find a nice selection for reasonable prices but I find a darling pink purse with Capri written on it. I just know that she will love that. At the same shop I am able to pick up a navy and white beach bag that says Capri but does not look tacky and is reasonable priced at ten euros. So I leave with something for myself as well.

Vincenzo is really nice and a perfect guide. He leads our small group, which he refers to as his family, up the "Mamma Mia" road to Anacapri in small buses. From there the panorama views are even more beautiful than from Capri. At Vincenzo's suggestion for a restaurant with authentic Italian food, I have lunch at *Barbarossa*, and then browse around the center of Anacapri. I find an internet point and am able to buy my train ticket from Salerno to *Boiano* for Friday.

On the bus ride back down to Capri and *Marina Piccolo*, the small marina, I meet two friendly guys from Vancouver. We use this time to share travel stories about our time in Italy. Before our ferry boat is due to leave, they kindly invite me to have a glass of wine with them at an outdoor restaurant and bar at the marina, my favorite kind of place.

I guess I will remember them forever since their names are David and Brian, the same as my sons' names. I really enjoy talking with them and hearing about their travel planning and accommodations they have arranged in the town of Minori, which sounds like another wonderfully quiet place. They refuse to allow me to pay for anything; they are such gentlemen. Thank you again, David and Brian, for the Pinot Grigio and great conversation. *Buon viaggio*, have a good trip, and maybe our paths will cross again one day in Mexico.

Instead of taking the boat to Amalfi and then riding the bus back to Maiori, I stay on the boat all the way back to Maiori. This morning, I now think, I could have taken this same ferry boat from the dock in Maiori, across the street from the monastery. I could have eliminated the bus trip to Amalfi too. But then, I remind myself, I would have missed that great experience of my bus backing down the street to make way for the oncoming one.

Back in Maiori, I walk down to the end of the promenade and find the ceramics shop I had read about, *Ceramica L'Arte Vietrese in Maiori*. The ceramics are from *Vietri*, ten kilometers from here, and the prices as well as the products and selection are excellent.

Pasquale, the owner, is very friendly and speaks English. I spend a lot of time conversing in English with him. When I hear him translate for his wife, *Maria,* I speak Italian so she can be included. Not only do they both treat me well as a customer, but as a human being as well. Both of them are so personable and I instantly like them. It is very apparent in the way Pasquale speaks of and treats his wife that he has great respect and love for her. And the nice interaction with them makes me want to stay here and just hang out. I buy a few small ceramic items I need for gifts, and then I cannot resist buying one more piece for myself. I will definitely return here before I leave Maiori just to say good-bye to Pasquale and his lovely wife.

On the way back to my room, I buy a slice of pizza and enjoy it as I walk along the *Lungomare,* or seafront, feeling the breeze against my face, watching waves gently rolling in from the sea, and watching all the families outside enjoying life. I am happy. After arriving back at *Casa di San Francesco* I sit on the veranda to write, with the smell of fresh lemons all around me. Again, it doesn't get much better than this.

This morning the sky looks like rain. I am so glad yesterday's excursion to Capri is a treasured memory instead of a soggy one. This is a good day to write and catch up on laundry. One of the nearby hotels, *Hotel San Francesco*, has Wi-Fi and the front desk manager is nice enough to let me use it for a reasonable fee as I sit in their lobby. I am able to catch up on my blog as well as my writing in a really nice atmosphere. While I am inside the hotel lobby, it rains again for several hours, so my timing cannot be any better. A few people who were on the boat to Capri yesterday are also in this hotel lobby, so we compare some of our impressions. I am happy to meet people who are as excited as I am about traveling in Italy.

Eventually the rain slows down to just a drizzle and I decide to head back to the ceramics shop in case I don't have a chance to visit tomorrow. I am disappointed that Maria is not there but within a short time she arrives, giving me a chance to take a photo with both of them. They are so down to earth and just genuinely nice people. I am so glad that I met them. I say my goodbyes but only after Pasquale gives me a special gift for good luck. He hands me a small, flat, and smooth coral-colored shell and explains that it is the *occhio di Santa Lucia*, eye of Saint Lucy. "*Questo guscio viene da un animale del mare*," repeating in English, "This shell comes from an animal of the sea," adding, "it can only be given as a gift." I am so very touched.

On the way home I decide to return to La Vela for dinner and treat myself to a glass of wine and marinara pizza. Once again, with compliments of the restaurant, I am treated to a *bibita*, a very refreshing drink made with orange, sugar, carbonated water, and lemon. And once again, the seaweed bruschetta appears at my table. I am sorry, but I cannot eat all this delicious food.

Back in my room I decide to go to sleep early, thanks to the wine. Tomorrow is a holiday when Italians celebrate the 150th anniversary of their country's unification. It will be interesting to see how a small town commemorates the event. Buona notte.

From the Amalfi Coast

to Colle d'Anchise

The weather forecast promises sunshine and warm temperatures. For me, that means a day at the beach. But first I walk to the nearby alimentaria where the shop owner is only too happy to make me a panini with great care and pride. I have to ask him to make it *piccolo*, as he is ready to pile a quarter pound of salami on it. "*Per favore, Signore, piccolo salami. Grazie,*" I say. Please, sir, little salami. Thank you. A section of fruit catches my eye while I wait and I select a nice red, ripe plum. After paying for my purchase, I say arriverderci and walk down the street toward the beach.

The fact I like about the small shops in these towns is that most are run by their owners. The difference is very noticeable, as they take great pride in what they are doing. They make sure the entry to their shops is swept, they greet you, and they are smiling as they prepare your order for you. Even the wrapping is not simple as they carefully package your purchase and tape it closed, sometimes even placing it into an additional bag. It's the little touches that make such a difference in their service.

Since it is a holiday here, more local people than usual are on the beach, and I love watching them. The young men, maybe eighteen or twenty years old, are singing. This is not something typically seen or heard on beaches in Florida, that is for sure. Italians love to sing, and although I was too young to remember, my older cousin, John, reminds me that my grandfather used to sing all the time. I wish I could remember that but he died when I was only nine. I do have fond memories of him, though, sitting outside under his apple tree and cutting up watermelon for my brothers and me to eat on hot summer afternoons.

The water here on the Amalfi Coast feels so refreshing, and even though these beaches are more rocky than sandy, I enjoy them. Because of their stones, however, I need my sandals to walk to the water. These hardy Italians are used to it and walk barefoot. I do love the scene of a beach surrounded by mountains of sheer rock that come right down into the ocean. It is an awesome sight, like a postcard, as Pasquale from the ceramics shop so accurately described. There really is no place quite like the Amalfi Coast; this is truly a place to which I could return year after year and never tire of it. After Rome this region is so relaxing. Since I leave in the morning, I make the most of my last day in Maiori.

This morning is my time to break away from this beautiful place. I am going to Boiano, the closest town with a train station, to see

Antonella and Michele. In contrast to the relaxation of yesterday, today will ultimately prove to be a day with a series of things going wrong. I guess after eight weeks in Italy, not every day is going to be perfect.

At breakfast, an older Italian man comes over to my table and strikes up a conversation. Yes, this is yet another man about seventy-five years old who starts talking to me, does not want to leave me alone, but offers to take me to Positano, Amalfi, and other places. He admits that he is married and his wife is not here with him. When I politely tell him I am leaving, he indicates that he wants to help me pack. He actually follows me to my room and when I tell him he cannot come with me, he pays no attention and I have to physically stop him before he finally walks away. What is it with these old Italian men? As much as I enjoy being on the Amalfi Coast, I think I am now ready to finish packing and get on the bus to Salerno as soon as possible.

As I check out from the monastery, I find out that I cannot pay by credit card, although the information states otherwise. Since I do not have enough cash to pay for five nights here, I now have to look for a Bancomat and withdraw money to pay them in cash prior to leaving. Okay, that really is not such a big problem. I know where the bank is and I have time before I have to board the bus to Salerno.

After paying my bill, I walk the short distance to the bus stop and wait for forty minutes in the hot sun, because the bus is twenty minutes late. When it arrives, it is packed with people and I have to get on with a suitcase. This immediately causes comments from one irate Italian woman. By this point, I run short on patience and have no plans to keep quiet. I board the bus with my luggage and say to her in Italian that I must get to the train station, *"Devo andare alla stazione ferroviaria,"* and nod toward my luggage. Luckily, a few stops later, many people get off and I find a seat as well as a place for my luggage. I do miss my own car more and more.

When I descend from the bus in Salerno, the other side of the strap on my luggage breaks.

The bus stops several blocks from the train station, so I have to ask directions a few times but at last arrive there. This day keeps going downhill, so keep reading.

I have an hour's wait at the train station where I notice a suspicious character hanging around, so I am now just a little more on guard than usual, but the wait, luckily, turns out to be uneventful. The trip to Boiano involves a change of trains in *Caserta.*

The train to Caserta departs from Salerno at 2:10PM. After about twenty minutes, the train suddenly stops and sits on the track for a half hour. Then it starts and moves slowly and after two or three minutes stops again. At no time does the engineer or any train personnel inform the passengers of what is happening. At 3:00PM, one of the passengers goes to the front and asks about the starts and stops. She finds out that there is a mechanical problem, and that the train will stop in another town called *Cancello*, where all the passengers will then board a bus to Caserta. By this time I had already missed the connecting train to Boiano, so I call Antonella to update her, since she is picking me up there. When the train arrives in Cancello, as promised, there is a bus provided by Trenitalia to Caserta. It is now almost 4:00PM.

The bus arrives near the train station in Caserta, and all of us have to walk in a light rain from the location the bus dropped us. Of course in the train station people are lined up to buy tickets, and only one window open. The person working there is in no hurry, but according to the departure board, no trains are leaving for Boiano anytime soon. I simply hope there will be a train sometime today, as I do not relish the idea of spending the night in Caserta. I must say my patience is wearing thin, and while waiting in line to adjust the train ticket, I can see an Italian girl not in line but positioning herself to move in front of me. As soon as she makes her move, I am ready and tell her, *"Io sono stata qui primo,"* I was here first, with a look that could kill, and it works. I am sorry, but with the day I am having, I am not putting up with her actions.

There is one bright spot to this day, though, and that is meeting an Australian family who was on the same train and later on the bus to Caserta. They are really friendly and we are sharing our frustrations of the day. They too were on the Amalfi Coast, but rather than taking a bus they paid a private driver to take them to the Salerno train station. They told me that what was supposed to be a forty-minute ride, took an hour and a half. This is Italy, and more specifically, the south of Italy, where efficiency is not on the agenda, whether you are in a bus, a private car, or a train.

Finally, at 5:45PM, I am on a train that is scheduled to arrive in Boiano at 7:30PM. Either Antonella or her husband, Michele, will pick me up. They are wonderful. I keep sending them several updates.

.

When I arrive in Boiano with no further delays, I see that it is Antonella, who is waiting for me with her car. I thank her and say, "I can't believe it took ten hours to travel a couple of hundred miles."

"Unbelievable. But the day isn't over, It will end on a good note," she says and drives me to the nearby village of Colle d'Anchise and to La Piano dei Mulini, my recent lodging with Rick and Monica. Antonella also makes a phone call to the priest, Don Fredy, and arranges for us to meet tomorrow at the church at 2:00PM. Things are looking up. At La Piano dei Mulini, my single room ends up to be a private apartment in a separate building. Everything here is so quiet, truly a welcome comfort after a stressful day. The whole interior of the apartment looks new and I can smell freshly stained cedar from the wooden beams on the ceiling. The entire place looks like a decorator's suggestion in a magazine.

Colle d'Anchise is in the Matese Mountains, so the air is actually cool here in the evenings and mornings. This is exactly what I need today. I feel like I am home again, in the village of my grandparents. After checking in and freshening up I decide to have a light dinner of just a salad in their restaurant and then call it a night...on a good note.

Buona notte.

I slept so well in my comfortable surroundings last night. And I am really happy to be back in Colle d'Anchise and to be staying at the comfortable La Piana dei Mulini in the countryside. This place is the perfect example of tranquility. I really love it here. This morning, during breakfast, I have the pleasure of meeting Signor Michele, the owner. He is actually coming over to sit down with me at my table. He speaks only Italian but we are able to have a nice exchange.

"I purchased this property about ten years ago," Signor Michele informs me in Italian during our conversation. If I understand correctly, he is also the cultural minister of this area and wants to maintain the natural beauty of this nineteenth-century original stone farmhouse while restoring it. A brochure states that this place was originally used for dyeing wool.

I also learn for the first time that this is not an agriturismo, as I had thought, but an *albergo diffuso*, a fairly new type of hospitality accommodation in Italy. Characterized as part house, part hotel, an albergo diffuso utilizes older structures, renovating them but keeping their unique characteristics. It typically consists of multi-use buildings spread out, maintaining the ambience and beauty of an area. What an interesting concept this is.

After breakfast, Antonella, Michele, and Gianluca arrive and drive me to the cemetery on *Campo Aperto*, where I spend the next two hours, curiously wandering through each section at my leisure, and reading the names I knew from my years of doing genealogy research. Ninety-nine percent of the monuments here are above ground with only a few older ones set lower. Those have markers, which can no longer be read, but interestingly there are fresh flowers at each one. The Italians take care of their people even long after they are gone, and now I understand even more why my grandmothers believed it was so important to make regular visits to the cemetery in Cleveland, where my grandfathers are buried.

The cemetery on Campo Aperto is so interesting to me. I notice that the monuments usually list the father's name and frequently have a picture of the buried person. Although I find several with my family's name, none are old enough to be the parents of my grandparents. I recall that Antonella had previously told me that the older graves no longer have monuments with names, which likely explains the absence of my great-grandparents' names.

An elderly man who lives next door to the cemetery happens to be sitting outside in his yard. When he sees me he motions for me to come over, inviting me to have something to drink, but I politely decline. After my previous experiences with old men here in Italy I am not looking for any more situations. In a town this small, anyone walking down the street invites curiosity, as the local people all know each other, most having lived here for their entire lives. He is probably lonely and just being nice, but I am not taking any chances.

It is now getting warm, despite the fact that the early morning was much cooler. So when I reach the small park near the statue of *Padre Pio*, I decide this is a good opportunity to take a break and sit down in the shade. While there, I notice some of the nearby homes have large piles of firewood, attesting to the fact that Colle d'Anchise is in the mountains and gets quite cold in the winter.

After wandering around the little village, taking photos, I eventually meet Antonella and her husband at her sister's small groceria. They are buying some items for lunch: salami, cheese, and prosciutto. Refusing to allow me to help pay for any of this, we leave the store when it is time to pick up Gianluca from school; together we go to their house for lunch.

It is comfortably cool in their house because of its thick walls of stone. Lunch is delicious. Afterward I play ball inside with Gianluca, who is a typical four-year-old boy who never stops moving. He is very cute. Antonella had told Michele about my broken luggage strap. He is able to find the right size screw and nut so I can repair the strap. Great!

At four thirty, Antonella and I meet with Don Fredy, the priest from the church where my grandparents were married. The appointment was supposed to be at two. He apologizes for the delay and mentions a forgotten earlier appointment.

The church of *Santa Maria degli Angeli* is beautiful with its tall, arched columns and frescoed ceiling. As I walk through it to the room where the records are kept, I have a keen awareness that I am walking in the same place where my grandparents and other ancestors walked years ago. This feels very special to me.

Don Fredy retrieves a number of record books, some of which are three hundred years old. When we find a marriage record for my grandparents, the month of their wedding is not the same that I expected. Also the name on the document is Carolina Baratta, but my grandmother's was Carmina Baratta. The rest of the data is the same, so we believe it to be the true record, but I am not one hundred percent positive. We are unable to find the other records I wanted, although, together, we look through many of the books. One book from the years 1812 to 1819 is missing. Even though I am here in person, this is not an easy task and I still don't have my grandfather's birth record. I am happy, however, to finally meet this priest and be able to see the church records. Don Fredy tells me that many people chose to marry in the cathedral of the neighboring town of Boiano. This may be why I have not been able to find the marriage records for my great-grandparents. Monday I will go to the municipio; I hope to have some luck there.

When I return to La Piana dei Mulini, I discover that they have Wi-Fi and are happy to give me the password. So I am thrilled to be connected again and be able to make a few Skype calls and a Face Time call to my family. The Wi-Fi signal only works outside but it is better than not having any signal at all. I realize that being connected while so far away, makes a huge difference to me.

At the close of the day, I enjoy a wonderful meal here and of course a glass of smooth, full-bodied red wine.

It is now Sunday morning. I like waking up with the cool breeze of the countryside entering through the open windows. La Piano dei Mulini feels like such a peaceful refuge.

This morning I have a chance to talk with Signor Michele about writing an article on La Piano dei Mulini. He is very involved in archeological projects in the region and is very interested in discussing some of this with me. He even takes time to show me a website on the computer, in Italian naturally, about his work. I plan to e-mail him from the States to interview him via the internet for the article. I would later realize that like so many other things, sometimes the best plans do not come to fruition and I would feel bad that I had not e-mailed him nor written the article, although I started it.

At ten o'clock Antonella and Gianluca come with her car to take me to the center of Colle d'Anchise so we can go to Mass. Antonella's sister, Santina, meets us in the street, and the four of us drive together to the parking area. We walk the short hill to the church of my grandparents where Antonella sings in the choir. Santina, Gianluca, and I sit in a pew and wait for Mass to begin. Of course the Mass is in Italian but I am used to this by now. I actually can understand some of Don Fredy's sermon and appreciate the value of those Italian lessons everyday. After Mass we are off to the home of Antonella's mother.

Isabella's entire family will be coming over at lunchtime. It is their family's tradition to spend Sundays together; it is also a way for the three sisters and their mother to catch up on common interests. Isabella works for a doctor and his family, taking care of his household all week, which she seems to enjoy. She prepares their meals, cleans, and does everything she would do for her own family. Isabella is such a positive person. I really like her.

I am grateful for her invitation two weeks ago to spend a Sunday with her family. I feel honored that she would include me on this special day.

When we arrive at her home, and before we even enter her kitchen, I recognize the wonderful, familiar smell of sauce cooking. Once inside, I see that she is busy working in her cucina. From the looks of it, Isabella must have been working since early in the morning. Everything simmering, bubbling, and baking smells even better at close range. She is making stuffed shells, eggplant, chicken, and judging from the many pots and pans, much more. She is smiling and seems very happy to prepare food for all of us.

I meet the whole family, including Santina's fiancé, *Marco*, and also *Pasqualina*'s husband, Giuseppe, and their teenage children. Pasqualina is the sister of Antonella's father, who lives in another part of Italy.

What starts out to be lunch turns into an all-day food event. Why am I not surprised at this? I am in Italy after all, Isabella loves cooking, and she just keeps bringing more food to the table, saying in English for my benefit, "It's just a little something." In addition to the stuffed shells, grilled eggplant, and baked chicken, there is home-made prosciutto, formaggio, salad, home-made wine, fruit, *pasticcia,* which is some type of sweet dessert from Pasqualina, and cream puffs and caffè.

All of us sit around the table for hours, and everyone except me, is talking fast and all at the same time, in typical Italian style. I am able to understand some, and can recognize when they are speaking dialect. Isabella lived for many years in Canada, so she speaks excellent English as well as Italian, which helps. I am thoroughly enjoying the animated conversations, even though I don't understand it all. I also love watching as they play Italian card games, *briscola* and *scopa.* I find it interesting that the men sit at one end of the table and the women at the other, even for the meal.

In the late afternoon, some of the family take me for a drive into the mountains to *Castelpetroso*, where we visit an impressive and stately Gothic cathedral. Two churches in one day, but this one is truly magnificent. "Rick, Monica, and I saw this huge church from the autostrada and wondered about it," I say. "This looks even more spectacular now that I am here." It is absolutely beautiful inside and out.

We spend some time inside the cathedral, named the Sanctuary of Sorrows of the Blessed Mary. After a few minutes in private prayer, I of course take some photos of the splendid altars and domed ceiling. Afterward, we get back into the car and drive further up into the mountains to an area close by the road, where I take photos of a tiny church as well as an outdoor shrine. I learn that here the Blessed Virgin Mary had appeared to two young shepherd girls, named *Bibiana* and *Serafina*, in 1888. Years later the Bishop of Boiano experienced an apparition here, and a miracle healing saved a young boy. A sign at the church indicates that Pope Paul VI proclaimed in 1973 that the Blessed and Sorrowful Virgin Mary would be the patroness of this region.

While we are at this higher elevation, I can feel that the air is much cooler here, even cold. I smell the fragrance of pine trees and the fresh scent of the mountain air.

"Oh, look! I can actually see some snow on a distant peak," I say. But then I fall silent, overcome by the beauty of the scenery and the absolute tranquility up here.

When we return to Isabella's house for a "snack," Isabella has more of the same food and then some, as though this was another full-course meal. Essentially it is another meal, although she calls it a snack and smiles. It is such a special experience for me to be able to share time with a family, really my own distant family of cousins, and I do get a sense of how the local Italian people live. This is not something most travelers to Italy ever encounter.

Besides all the other food that I have already tasted, Isabella serves pomodoro, bruschetta, *tartuffo,* truffle, watermelon, cantaloupe, popcorn, and ice cream too, and of course more vino! This is the first time that I have truffles. Apparently, in Colle d'Anchise everyone goes out truffle hunting. There are even special truffle dogs kept for that purpose. As a bruschetta the truffles taste delicious. They are very expensive to purchase, so they usually are served in a small quantity such as a topping for bruschetta, which Isabella makes.

I am having such a wonderful time and really feel like part of their family. At the end of the day, just before nine, Michele and Carolina drive me back to La Piano dei Mulini. I feel so happy.

.

Searching for Records before

Moving on

It's my last morning in Colle d'Anchise and after packing my bags and savoring my breakfast, I am ready to check out and say grazie and arrivederci to Signor Michele. I really like him and this morning I have the good fortune to meet his lovely young wife. They make a beautiful couple.

Antonella is here to take me to the *comune*, town hall, where I am hoping to locate some records of my father's family, particularly my grandfather's birth record. As of now I am still unable to find it.

At the comune, however, I quickly become disappointed because the woman at the desk informs us that she is too busy to search any records for me. I am so grateful for Antonella's presence. She patiently explains to me that this woman is a secretary and is not the one who usually searches the records. Instead there is a man, an *anagrafi*, researcher, whose job it is to locate the requested records. If we can find him, he will be the one to help us. Luckily, he appears at that very moment and, by coincidence, he is Pasqualina's brother-in-law. Small towns definitely have their benefits sometimes.

He indicates for us to follow him to the location of the record room. Once inside this room I get an idea of how mammoth a job it may be to find the records that I am looking for here. This man, whose name is *Giacomo Lombardi*, is a saint because he is not only very friendly but also extremely helpful and patient. He spends quite a bit of time with us and locates some birth records from 1816 as well as verifying births to 1792. There are no records in Colle d'Anchise, though, that go back as far as 1792, with the earliest being 1815, which is not surprising to me. In my years of genealogy research, the records for Italy do not go back much further either. I appreciate the information he does find, and also Antonella's help in translating and communicating for both of us.

From what Signor Lombardi is able to find, the birth record I had hoped to uncover, the one of my grandfather, *Roberto Longano*, is unfortunately not here. It looks like *Campobasso* may be where his 1884 birth was registered. Since his marriage record states that he lived in Colle d'Anchise, but was born in Campobasso, Giacomo says that the record must be in Campobasso. I will have to e-mail the municipio there and see if they can locate it. After we leave the records room, Antonella drives to Don Fredy's house so I can drop off a thank-you note in his mailbox along with a small donation to the church. Then she takes me to the train station in Boiano, about five miles away. I have thoroughly enjoyed my time in the village of my Longano grandparents.

With a couple of hours to wait for the train, I have an opportunity to write at a tiny outdoor table while having something cold to drink. Boiano's railroad station is very small. It is just a place for the trains to stop. Today is going to be a long travel day, since there are three trains involved to arrive in *Ostuni*, which is in the heel of Italy, in *Puglia*. I hope there will be no mechanical problems on the trains today. The first one, from Boiano to Caserta, goes smoothly. There I quickly locate my next one on which I have a reserved seat. This train is full and a man is already sitting in my seat and insists he is not moving.

I later realize that I should have said nothing but tried to find another seat, maybe even in another car. Instead I speak to the train authority, a woman, about my problem. After reviewing my ticket she informs me that it is invalid because I have mistakenly bought it for the wrong date. So I am the one who is wrong, not the man in the seat. I am completely embarrassed and very humbled immediately, yet at the same time understand that I am in a dilemma.

The woman explains to me that I can get off the train at the next stop and buy another ticket, an option I definitely do not like since I have no idea when the next connections might be. My other option is to pay an additional fifty euros on the train now. She tells me to find a seat for now and informs me that she will be back. With luck, I find a seat and start saying Hail Mary's, partly because I feel bad for making a scene, and partly hoping that she will not be back to check the ticket. Anyway this is a three-hour train ride and by a stroke of good luck I never see the woman again, or anyone else to check the ticket. During my trip in Italy, I learn more than ever to never underestimate the power of prayer.

A kind gentleman sitting next to me on this train warns me to remove my jewelry before arriving in *Bari*, because people have been known to pull it off. I immediately do as he suggests, remembering warnings from my son, David, about Bari being dangerous because of pickpockets. At the Bari station, I quickly locate my binario, and immediately go there to wait for my train to Ostuni. I make sure to be even more aware of my surroundings than I normally am, and everything turns out to be fine. On the train to Ostuni, the conductor checks the tickets, but mine is fine for this part of the trip. Thank you, God!

In Ostuni I find a shuttle bus to take me to the centro storico for eighty euro cents. The driver promises to drop me off right in front of my hotel. Always eager to speak Italian I meet a very likeable nineteen-year-old, petite Italian girl named *Lucia* on the bus. She speaks English very well and tells me that she works in a pub near the cathedral. I tell her I will see her again and make a mental note of her description of the name and location of the pub. She comes from *Brindisi* and has recently moved to Ostuni because she was able to find a job here.

Just as the driver said, the shuttle bus stops in front of the *Ostuni Palace*, which looks inviting. After an easy check-in, I decide on dinner in their restaurant, trying a local specialty, *fazzoletti*, which is homemade pasta, made with buckwheat and shaped like ravioli. The little ravioli are filled with ricotta cheese and *pancetta*, bacon, and mixed with tomatoes and arugula. It is very tasty.

The Ostuni Palace is a wonderful hotel. It feels good to be here after a long travel day yesterday. I am eager to explore the town, especially since this region of Italy is new to me. Ostuni is where Angela and Teresa's sister-in-law, Monica, grew up; Angela recommends that I base myself here while I am visiting Puglia.

I am out to explore Ostuni, and just outside my hotel I discover that I have a fantastic view of the old part of this city. I understand why it is called *Città Bianca*, the white city. From where I am standing, I can see the entire center of Ostuni perched on a hill; it looks striking with all the white houses and buildings.

The walk to the centro is short, maybe ten or fifteen minutes away. There are photo opportunities around every corner, especially since it is early and not too many people are out yet. The cathedral is one of the main landmarks in Ostuni and of course I want to check it out. It is a fifteenth-century Romanesque-Gothic style church dedicated to the Madonna of the Assumption. The façade is really beautiful with its ornate, intricately crafted rose windows. I decide to go inside, paying the one euro donation. No cathedral ever disappoints in Italy as they are all such architectural masterpieces, and this one is no exception.

While browsing around the narrow alleys near the cathedral, I happen to run into Lucia, the girl on the shuttle bus. I am really happy to see her and she offers to show me her house, which is right around the corner. It is tiny but spotless and meets her needs. Inside it is cool because the small accommodation is built entirely of stone. Everything is in one room except for a tiny but separate bathroom.

Actually, for a nineteen year-old girl to be living on her own and supporting herself in southern Italy, where jobs are not plentiful, she is doing great. I am totally impressed with her motivation when she tells me she wants to be independent. Lucia, you already are independent, supporting yourself in your own apartment away from home. Showing me a small bag of candies that she bought yesterday, she offers me some. Here is someone who does not have much but yet she is offering me some of what she does have. What a kind and giving person she is. I really like her a lot and find myself wanting to root for her to do well.

Her traditional Italian parents do not approve of her living away from their house. I encourage her, explaining that if she can get an education, she has a good chance of doing well. Her story is inspiring and reminds me of a time when my son Brian moved to New York City at the age of twenty. As a parent I didn't think then that it was too inspiring, but years later I realize that it took a lot of courage to do something like that. Go, Lucia! Later I will find out that Lucia is planning on applying for the nursing program at the university. I wish her the best and know she will do well.

I spend the afternoon in my hotel doing some writing, catching up on laundry, and making plans for the next few days in Puglia. I also discover the great rooftop view from my hotel!

The time is eleven thirty at night and I am getting ready to go to bed. After this day of varied activities I am tired. Suddenly I hear this horrific noise from the bathroom and within an instant, water seems to be flowing everywhere. Apparently a pipe has burst and hot water is just pouring out of it. In Italy there are these radiator/hot water heaters that are attached to the wall. They look like ladders. I can see that a piece of it had broken off, causing the water to be gushing all over. I cannot see any way to shut off the water and immediately call the front desk for help.

Within minutes the bathroom as well as the bedroom is flooded. I immediately close the door to the bathroom and start to stuff towels beneath the opening to help reduce further flooding. Two men who work at the reception desk appear at my door. They are dressed in suits and of course are completely useless except for being able to contact the engineer who is of course off site. The men open the linen closet in the hallway and happily produce more towels for me to use as a barrier while we wait for the engineer. I am sure they are happy to not have to enter the flooded room with their expensive leather dress shoes.

What I am even more horrified to realize and what I certainly do not want the hotel personnel to find out is that my laundry is pinned to the makeshift clothesline, which is attached to that radiator. I would not think that it should cause a pipe to break, but I certainly am not volunteering this information. Now, however, I will have to rewash everything tonight. So much for an early bedtime! One of these men, who must be the front desk manager, tells me to pack up my things and he will move me to another room as soon as I am ready. It does not take me long to gather my belongings and transfer them to the room next door. The upside to this saga is that I now have a room with a view of the centro.

Puglia is not known for being a major tourist area compared to Rome, Florence, and Venice, but many Italians and Europeans come here during the summer. It is not that easy to travel to the small towns without a car, so I arrange with the front desk to have a private driver arrive to take me to the towns in this area where the *trulli,* conical shaped houses, are found. The trulli are the main reason I put Puglia on my itinerary. So today I visit *Martina Franca, Alberobello,* and *Cisternino.*

I am ready at 8:15AM when *Angelo* comes in a minivan to collect and drive me through the *campagna,* countryside, from Ostuni to Martina Franca. Although Angelo speaks only Italian, we are able to communicate with no problem.

Within ten minutes I catch my first glimpse of the trulli. They are dotting the countryside more and more as we drive the forty-five minutes to Martina Franca. The only way to see this area is by car; there is no question about that, as we are definitely into the countryside.

In Martina Franca, Angelo drops me off at the centro and I now have an hour and a half to walk around and explore on my own. Before I go anywhere, I take a minute to notice where I am and take a few photos of landmarks and street signs to use as guideposts. This way I will be able to show them to someone in case I lose my bearings and ask for help to find my way back to this drop-off point. I have done this a few times already on this solo adventure; it seems to work well for me. Traveling solo I don't have the luxury of relying on travel partners for navigation advice so this method is a good one for me. I am not nervous and do not worry that I may not know how to get back.

I notice that this town is exceptionally clean. I love the stone alleys and narrow streets with flowers on the steps. Although Martina Franca is not one of the towns that has the trulli within the walls of the town, I find the centro charming with its piazzas. I am glad I selected this town as part of today's itinerary. The eighteenth-century basilica of baroque design is gorgeous with its rich ornaments. When I walk inside, a Mass is being celebrated. The ample use of marble in the interior is amazing to behold.

I don't see any other tourists around and while exploring the streets, I find a man cleaning his vegetables out of his truck next to the small shop where they are sold. I love this scene as I really am able to see how the local people live every day. I imagine this man sees few tourists like me so he is more than happy to allow me to capture this memory with my camera. *Grazie*! I have time to stop in at *Gran Caffè* and use the bathroom, which is upstairs, and then have a Coca Light outside before I meet Angelo.

Angelo is waiting for me at the agreed time. Next, he drives me to Alberobello, the main town of the unique homes, the trulli. In fact Alberobello is designated as an official UNESCO location. As Angelo says, "*Tanti trulli in Alberobello.*" There are many trulli in Alberobello. These homes are old and are no longer being built, so they are much in demand and expensive, according to Angelo. There is even a trullo-shaped *chiesa*, church, *la chiesa a trullo*. All trulli are built completely out of stone; the stones are laid one on top of the other. Inside, these dwellings are cool, due to their corbeled dry masonry. They characteristically have dome-shaped roofs and can only be found in the Puglia region of Italy. What makes them interesting is that they were built so that they could be quickly disassembled and the people could avoid being taxed.

From my reading I learn that Alberobello is sort of a tourist trap, and it actually is. There are numerous small shops that are also trulli, and the shopkeepers sit outside, encouraging me and the many other tourists to enter and buy something. This town is not like Martina Franca, where I was the only tourist. I don't care for this aspect of Alberobello.

Although the shopkeepers are engaging, they are selling the same items that I can buy in Ostuni for two or three euros, but here they ask five or six euros. Some unique handmade items made out of stone, miniature trulli homes, are created by local artisans. These are probably worth buying.

Aware that I only have a limited amount of time here, I move about the town pretty quickly, and after an hour here, I see Angelo and his minivan. Time to proceed to Cisternino. On the way, he stops on the side of the road so I can take a few photos of the trulli that are in the countryside. Once we arrive in Cisternino, I again have an hour to spend, so I check out the basilica, the Church of St. Nicolas of Patara, which dates back to the sixteenth century. Then I wander around the small streets, again aware of where I am going, because there is a distinct possibility that I could get lost here. I also find the very tiny Church of St. Lucia that has only one room and measures five by six meters.

When I feel hungry, I ask a local woman to recommend a place to eat, since I don't see too many restaurants that are open. She suggests *Trattoria Bere Vecchie* and even gives me directions as to its location. As I walk inside, I have to pass by the small kitchen and can see three people preparing the food and getting ready for lunch. It feels so intimate to me. I like this wonderful spot immediately because it is small and full of local character.

At present I am the only customer in the restaurant. The ambience is perfect, right down to the hand paintings on the walls. I order a pasta dish specific to this region, *orchiette*, small pasta shaped like an ear, with a pomodoro sauce and fresh formaggio. The pasta is of a dark color, similar to the buckwheat pasta at the hotel restaurant. In addition to pane the pleasant waiter also serves me some sautéed zucchini, as well as a raw vegetable plate, all complimentary. This is the most delicious lunch. Including a liter of aqua naturale, the bill is ten euros and well worth it.

Afterward Angelo returns me to my hotel, where I relax and actually take a nap for the first time on this trip. I would not trade today for anything.

Ostuni and Puglia

At the front desk, a clerk kindly arranges a taxi for me to the private beach recommended by the hotel. One of the deciding factors for me to stay in Ostuni is its proximity to the Adriatic Sea. The city has a population of around thirty-two thousand but in the summer months it can swell to a hundred thousand people, mainly because of the beaches. Today is a beautiful sunny day, and I can't wait to relax on a strand, which is calling my name.

Although I can see the coast from my hotel room window, in reality the shore is not that close and almost impossible to reach without a car. No public transportation is available to the seaside, and from what I understand, most of the beaches have private accesses. The hotel has an arrangement with *Viar Beach Club,* and for half a day the cost is fifteen euros for access to the beach, a beach umbrella, and two lounge chairs. That price is not too bad, but then the taxi is twenty-five euros round trip. *Amo la spiaggia.* I love the beach. And since this is a perfect weather day, the cost is just part of the vacation in Ostuni.

At 10:30AM the taxi arrives right on schedule and soon I understand why private transportation is necessary, and why I can't walk to the beach from the hotel. The taxi ride to the beach takes only fifteen minutes but the area is quite remote. To reach the beach club property, we have to drive on a dirt road past rows and rows of olive trees and not much of anything else. Olive trees are in abundance in the Puglia region, with more than sixty million of them today. Producing approximately forty percent of Italy's olive oil, Puglia cultivates groves of olive trees on more than a third of all the Italian land that has been set aside for olive growing. The familiar light olive-green color of the leaves can be seen for miles.

Once in a while I can see olive trees that have very wide trunks, which are twisted into gnarly shapes. I see this type of old olive trees for the first time. They are the *ulivi secolari,* olive trees that are literally centuries old, some of them even more than a thousand years. In Puglia, four million olive trees are over three hundred years old, and of all the olive trees in Puglia, half of them have produced fruit for more than a hundred years.

Soon we arrive at Viar Beach Club. It amazes me that something so luxurious can exist in this remote rural setting. This beach complex is situated among sea oats and other natural shrubs, which grow close to the ocean. The walkways and signs are made of wood; the atmosphere is casual yet sophisticated.

Since it is not yet tourist season here, the Viar Beach Club is not at all crowded. Apparently my hotel has a close communication with the club manager here, because I am surprised to find him waiting for me with a warm welcome. Young and pleasant, *Donato* greets me in English and points me toward the beach, which is absolutely beautiful. A sandy beach without rocks is a rare pleasure for me in Italy. The water is crystal clear and pleasing to the eye with its shades of green, turquoise, and royal blue. It is eleven in the morning and I am in heaven, totally enjoying my day at Viar Beach Club. This place is fabulous and it is so worth the entrance fee and taxi fare. I can envision spending several days right here. How relaxing this is!

After soaking up the sun and the sand for several hours, it is time to go. According to the hotel reception desk clerk, I would not find a cab waiting here to take me back. "Ask the taxi driver to return for you." I can believe it now that I see the location, so I am glad for that advice.

While I wait for the taxi at two in the afternoon, I drink a Coca Light at the bar, and have the pleasure of talking with the manager of this property. Donato is fit and attractive and lives here with his wife. He continues to work at making this beach resort into a first-class establishment. Guests have numerous options for relaxation and fun, such as massage, volleyball, tennis, and soccer.

"On weekends," Donato says, "our three bars and the restaurant are very busy, especially from July until September, which is our tourist season."

Donato is very welcoming and even extends to me the use of his computer if I need it. He is very up-to-date with his business, as he has a website and a Facebook page. I take notice how he speaks with pride about his plans for the beach club. He shows me around and explains that the jacuzzi and swimming pool are almost finished and will be ready for the busy summer season. Obviously he is a good businessman.

When I return to the hotel, I am hungry and order a salami panini at their outdoor café, enjoying a little more of this glorious sun. After a while I head back to my room to take a shower and do some photo editing and writing. I am glad that I am in Italy with the time built in for relaxation. Usually on a trip, it is go, go, go, and when I return home, I feel like I need a vacation. To have this amount of time here is gratifying. Working as a nurse in a busy critical-care unit, it is almost impossible to be able to take more than two or three weeks off at a time.

One reason I like to plan my own itinerary and time schedule when I come to Italy, rather than take an organized tour, is to be able to take time for relaxation like I do today. The tours are nice for someone who has never been to a particular place, but they pack a lot in, so that participants have very little time to relax. On occasion, in some of the hotels in which I stay on this trip, I see crowds of tourists that are on organized tours, waiting together in hotel lobbies to get checked in, or waiting outside for a bus. This is not for me; I am glad I have the opportunity to do my own thing.

This evening I head out to the centro to find the pub *Gipas 111*, where Lucia works. I recall Lucia saying on the bus there is no sign for the pub, but I know that it is located somewhere behind the cathedral. After wandering around in that area for a bit, I end up asking some men, "*Scusi, dove è Bar Gipas 111?*" Excuse me, where is Bar Gipas 111? And it is right in front of me.

This pub is a cool place, very modern with its purple and black triangular, stuffed fabric chairs outdoors. They seem to be very comfortable and are of a new design for me on this trip. I like them.

Bar Gipas 111 used to be an old bakery. Since it is early in the evening and Lucia isn't busy, she has time to give me a tour. Showing me around the bar, she explains that the original oven is now used to store the bottles of liquor and wine. She even shows me the bathroom and tells me that it is also her job to clean it. It seems that Bar Gipas only has two employees, *Antonio,* the manager, and Lucia. The place has a great ambience and looks like a good spot to spend an evening. I order a glass of red wine and talk some more with Lucia.

This nineteen-year-old young woman has not had an easy upbringing, living with a foster family for quite a few years. She has a younger brother whom she cares about very much. After she shares with me some of her struggles and frustrations concerning family problems, I can understand even better how she developed this sense of independence. She is smart and has goals. I think she will reach them one day. For her age, Lucia is wise already.

Business seems to pick up in the bar now that it is getting later, and Lucia has more customers to serve. "I should leave and let you do your work," I say. "We'll stay in touch. I'll write to you from America."

"Oh please. I will answer you with news from Italy. Now we are friends."

After I leave Bar Gipas 111, I walk downhill in the direction of an outdoor trattoria that I remember looked inviting earlier. At *La Reggia Ristorante* umbrellas cover the tables, which is good since it is starting to drizzle. I feel like an Italian, eating late and enjoying some pasta pomodoro, of course, and the special bread product from this region, *taralli*. These are small, crunchy, ring-shaped snacks similar to crackers or pretzels, predominantly found in southern Italy. As I walk home after dinner, I smile, happy to be in Italy.

Only an hour from Ostuni by train, the city of *Lecce* is my destination for today. Already on my way to the train station, I eagerly anticipate my visit to that city in southern Puglia. I have it on my itinerary, because I follow the suggestions of friends who know of its reputation as the Florence of the South. Lecce earns this honor mainly because of its many old churches and palaces that have the elaborate baroque style of architecture, as well as the ornate monuments.

In Lecce I take a local bus to the centro storico and get ready to explore, camera in hand. Just as I have made a habit of doing in other towns, I take a few photos with my iPhone of the area where I alight from the bus, so I can find my way back later.

The centro storico seems fairly large; in my opinion it is the size of Florence. The city looks very clean; its streets are paved with stone. One of the major differences between Lecce and Florence is the lack of crowds here. Puglia has only recently been discovered as a tourist destination, so anywhere you go, there are less people than farther north. Since I prefer smaller places, I really enjoy the town of Lecce, where I can wander around at my leisure and shoot photos of landscapes and street scenes without a lot of people in the shot.

I have a map of Lecce, so I have some idea of what I am seeing on this self-guided tour through the old town. So many of the buildings are incredible examples of art in architecture. One of the most interesting landmarks is a first-century BC Roman amphitheatre at *Piazza Sant' Oronzo*. In the same area is the seventeenth century ninety-five-foot-tall column with a statue of Sant' Oronzo, the patron saint of Lecce, at the very top.

Piazza Duomo is the site of the beautiful cathedral of Lecce with a bell tower that is over 160 feet tall. Like so many of the other monuments here, the cathedral was built in the seventeenth century, but previously other ancient churches had been on the site. The interior is an awesome sight with its twelve altars in addition to the main altar; each of these is a work of art. Other buildings, including a seminary, complete this piazza, where an art lover could spend an entire day.

I prefer to wander around, continuing to be amazed at the buildings. I definitely understand why the Lecce people are proud of their city.

At lunchtime, I try one of their *prodotti tipici*, typical food products from the town. This type of bread is orange in color because it is made with pomodori; it also contains some onions and many olives. The shop owner is nice enough to warn me about biting into the bread because of the olive pits. I presume, that to give the bread such an intense flavor it is necessary to use the whole olive. I like it; it is a good snack to eat as I walk around. I can taste the sweetness of olive oil, which gives the bread a delicious flavor.

While I continue to browse the streets, I encounter someone asking for money, as is typical in almost every place I visit. "*Fame?*" I ask if he is hungry and give him the rest of the bread. I think he expected money and the look of surprise will remain a memory for me forever, but he accepts the food and eats it almost immediately.

June is very warm in the south of Italy and most of the regional trains are not air-conditioned. Before I reach the bus stop, I find a beautiful park with benches and a lot of trees. This peaceful green setting is perfect for taking a break after walking around all day in the heat. I choose one of the benches to rest for a few minutes and take in the scenery and the people around me. On another bench sits a young couple who seem happy to be together. I finish drinking a bottle of water during my respite, then walk the few hundred yards to the bus stop.

By late afternoon I am on the train back to Ostuni and upon arrival, I take the local bus to the centro and my hotel, the Ostuni Palace, which is a luxurious lodging to spend five days. After every busy day I like to return to my temporary base. The lobby, where I spend evenings keeping record of my activities, is inviting and charming in design with its colors of vibrant green and subtle gold. Overstuffed chairs, arranged in several sitting areas make this a comfortable place. Another section of the lobby is toward the direction of the bar where there is always a bartender on duty.

I find the lobby to have a tranquil atmosphere. And this evening I do some more writing where I have come to feel very much at home. Here I use the Wi-Fi here it has the best connection, and edit and upload my photos while I am in Italy. It is actually relaxing for me to do this and I am glad I have the time for it. Before I go back upstairs to my room, I talk with the front desk receptionist and make arrangements for a taxi to the airport tomorrow, because I want to fly to Milan, and then go to Lake Como from there. Bari airport is not close by and the cost is eighty euro, but it is worth it to me. I would rather take a plane than arrive at the Bari train station again, since I remember the warnings about it being a dangerous place.

I have two and a half weeks left in Italy and hope to continue to enjoy this ride. I realize that I have an opportunity like no other and savor every experience. During my entire stay in Italy, every day is a learning opportunity about the Italian people and also about my own capabilities.

Although I am blogging about my experiences, I want to write a much more detailed account about this solo travel adventure and how it impacts my life.

There are certain aspects of daily life in Italy that make an indelible mark in my mind and change my perspective on life in many ways. Maybe more than anything else, I am inspired by the hardiness of the older Italian men and women. In many places of Italy, their houses are built into hillsides, which might offer great views, but also necessitate walking up and down hundreds of uneven stone steps every time they go anywhere. In some small villages, even if someone owns a car, the person may have to park it on a street two hundred feet below the house and walk home the rest of the way.

Italians living in the mountainous areas do this every day. In all kinds of weather they carry anything they buy or need to take with them, when they leave their homes. In some regions, their homes may be along the street, but the street could be on a thirty-degree incline or more, as well as the numerous other streets they must maneuver to reach a bus line, the chiesa, or small groceria.

This is their way of life, though, so they do it without complaining or asking for help. It definitely makes me think twice before complaining over trivial inconveniences, such as not having a close parking spot at the supermarket. Being here is a life-altering experience for me and I know that I will return home and be a changed person. I am grateful for this insight and learning experience.

Going to Lake Como

This travel day sees me cross hundreds of miles from the heel of Italy north to Lake Como. I have the good luck of meeting a young taxi driver named *Marco,* who speaks English and Italian. The ride to the airport in Bari is comfortable and picturesque as Marco points out places along the coast and also validates for me what I have heard about crime in Bari.

Marco is married and has two children. Both he and his wife work due to these economically hard times. They live here in Ostuni but he is from the neighboring town of Martina Franca. If he were not married, he would be expected to live in the same town as his parents. Thus our conversation leads to a discussion of the concept of *Mammoni,* the idea of Italian men living with their mothers until they are married or of middle age. I love to talk to young people here and hear their perspective on matters that I have only learned about through reading. Much of it seems to be true.

Thanks to our animated discourse, the time passes quickly and in an hour I am at the airport and say goodbye to Marco.

My flight to Milan is uneventful, and from Milan it is only an hour by train to *Varenna,* where I will be staying on Lake Como for five days of relaxation. I arrive in Varenna in the early afternoon and nothing pictured in brochures can compare to the beauty of *Lago di Como* before my eyes. The lake is completely surrounded by mountains with small villages and towns around the shore and into the hills. It is an extremely tranquil setting, perfect for relaxing and writing, as well as providing some awesome photo opportunities.

My hotel, the *Eremo Gaudio,* is situated high into a hill, and from my window the view of the lake as well as the small medieval village of Varenna is breathtaking. Varenna, which is at the bottom of a steep hillside, has only eight hundred residents and is not as commercialized as *Bellagio* across the lake. It does have a ferry boat dock, from which you can take either passenger ferries or others that transport cars and passengers to Bellagio, *Menaggio, Como,* and more towns around the lake.

After checking into the hotel, I walk the ten minutes downhill into the center of town to go exploring. I find the main piazza and discover that it is named after one of the four churches, *San Giorgio.* To have four churches in one piazza in a town this small is surprising. Next, I locate one of the narrow, steep *contradas,* alleys, which descends to the level where there are small shops and restaurants, but only a few people.

I am in the mood for a slice of margherita pizza and choose a little restaurant along the lake with outdoor tables and umbrellas.

As I sit outside at the *Nilus Bar* in Varenna, listen to the crested waves hitting the shoreline, and watch the ferry cross the lake to Bellagio, I am again aware of one of my peculiarities: More than at any other place, I love to be near the water. Whether it is an ocean, a lake, or a marina, the water is always the place where I feel completely relaxed and happy. I look out at sailboats that are anchored close to the shore and observe the mallard get shooed away by a waiter. The sounds of the waves drown out any of the conversations from nearby tables. Clouds settle after an early morning rain in the lower mountains surrounding the lake. Sometimes I think it wouldn't take too much to keep me here, but when I awaken from my daydream, I instantly remember the stark realities of life on a hillside in Italy. Besides, I live in Florida, a peninsula…without mountains, though.

After my tasty lunch and time to indulge in a daydream, I find my way to the *passarella*, the stone walkway close to the lake. Along the passageway, the views of the lake and surrounding hillsides are even more beautiful than my first glimpse. Varenna is a lovely little town with its winding streets, steep staircases, and small shops. It also is very quiet. I check out the farmacia, which by luck is open, but, since it is Monday, the small *salumeria*, a delicatessen that sells cured meats, is closed. I will have to return tomorrow when it is open. As I walk around again on the upper piazza area, a light rain starts and I duck inside the *Chiesa San Giorgio,* Church of Saint George, which is very pretty. This fourteenth-century church is beautiful inside with its many works of art and frescoes. I especially like that it has a tall bell tower, which rings every hour and also on the half hour during daytime.

Before I walk back uphill to my hotel, I must stop and have some gelato, and on the recommendation of the person working in the gelato shop, I try cinnamon for the very first time. The taste is really good; there is a distinct possibility that it may be replacing pistachio as my favorite gelato flavor. The friendly young woman behind the counter speaks English. I learn that she is from Russia and has lived here for seven years. I find myself wondering how she ended up here.

When I continue my way back to my hotel, I get some extra unplanned exercise as I miss the road going up the hillside. Instead I walk practically to the next village and have to backtrack. I can't understand how that could happen but I guess my sense of direction is not that great here. It is still raining lightly, so, despite having an umbrella, by the time I get to the hotel, I am soaked. Within an hour, though, the sun comes out again.

The friendly hotel clerk speaks good English, so I engage her in conversation about restaurants in Varenna before going out for my evening meal. "What restaurant would you recommend for dinner?" She suggests the small quiet establishment *Isola Nuova*, saying it is situated near the lake. She adds that in northern Italy the dinner time is earlier than in the southern region where Italians do not think of eating dinner before nine. Thus northern restaurants serve dinner earlier and do not stay open as long either.

I walk back into town and down one of the contradas to the lakeside where I find the lovely restaurant, Isola Nuova, almost hidden by green foliage, which presents a colorful setting. The food is good but no better than at many of my previous stops in Italy. After dinner I walk back, but take the short way this time.

The lake looks so peaceful with its surroundings so scenic; it makes me feel as though I never want to leave. Breakfast on the outdoor terrace is as relaxing as I can wish, and this morning I have the pleasure of meeting a nice couple, Dean and Nancy, from Colorado. This is their second trip to Lake Como and they too consider it a scenic and tranquil place.

Since I am traveling alone, I am happy to meet other people from time to time, especially if they speak English. Sometimes I meet Americans and other times, the people are from the U.K. or Australia. They are always very friendly. It is fun swapping stories and, thus, we learn from one another about places we are either going to or coming from in Italy. I never feel alone here even though I am traveling solo.

The Eremo Gaudio has several levels; the higher levels are reached through a series of lifts or funiculars. My room is on the lower level, but Dean and Nancy are staying in one of the rooms on the higher level. They are happy to give me a tour. There is a locked entrance to the funicular and all guests are allowed access, but it is not that simple to figure out how to run it. So I am happy for the personal, guided tour. They show me how to operate the lift and tell me how the views from the higher levels are even more awesome than from my room and the terrace. My earlier decision to spend the day sitting outside, relaxing, and enjoying the views, is now intensified by what I see from the higher levels. I am so glad I chose this hotel.

My research about Hotel Eremo Gaudio explains that it originally served as a hermitage for priests and later as an orphanage. The *Pirelli* family had it built. Then they donated the building to the church, since one of their sons was a priest. The structure was only recently made into a hotel with twenty-one rooms on six levels.

The people who work here are extremely accommodating, making sure that I enjoy my cappuccino on the terrace, as well as the views of Lake Como.

In the afternoon I take a walk into town and all along the passarella down to the ferry landing. This elevated walkway is out over the water and very peaceful. Some people call it the Lover's Walk and I can see that a stroll might be very romantic, especially at night.

Back at the hotel, I have dinner outside on the terrace. The burgundy-and-white-colored tablecloths and the fresh pink geraniums in the flowerboxes along the terrace railing add to the ambience of the lake view. I am having *melanzane alla parmigiana*, eggplant parmesan, which tastes absolutely delicious, thanks to Italians' expertise in cooking. And, of course, with the accompaniment of a glass of wine.

I make, however, a thought-provoking observation: the restaurant is out of pasta pomodoro, although it is listed on the menu. The Italian restaurateurs have an unusual way of informing you that they are out of an item. Instead of saying, "We are out of that," they say "It is finished," or "*È finito.*" I hear this occasionally, and because these eateries are so small, they will not receive any deliveries until perhaps the following week. So it is possible that on a Monday they are out of a simple menu item, such as pasta pomodoro, for an entire week. And that is just the way it is. In America for example, restaurant customers are not used to that and would never put up with it; they might even go to another restaurant. But in Italy customs are different, and I learn to be more flexible while here.

Nancy and Dean join me later and tell me about their day in Bellagio. I plan to take the ferry to visit there tomorrow as the weather forecast looks good.

Now that I know my way around Varenna, I go down to the town dock and take the ferry over to Bellagio this morning. The views of Varenna from the water are picturesque. As the ferry is approaching Bellagio, I have a chance to capture some great landscape shots of this colorful resort town. I can also see Eremo Gaudio high up on the hillside from across the lake.

The waterfront looks like a postcard, with all the colorful shops and hotels lined up next to each other in a perfect way. Bellagio is beautiful but much more commercialized than Varenna, with numerous shops and restaurants at the waterfront and up and down the many narrow stone staircases. It is very clean, like Varenna, and there is a sense of good taste with all the shops. None are tacky, even though this is a tourist town. Some items are quite expensive, however; for example, the cookies in a pasticceria are priced at twenty-five euros per kilogram. With today's exchange rate of almost $1.50 that comes to about seventeen dollars a pound.

Approximately twenty minutes on foot away from the town center is a small fishing village called *Pescallo*. To reach this quaint village, I have to navigate one of the various staircases in Bellagio; they are called *salita,* which means hill. Rather than finding street names here, I read signs of named staircases, such as *Salita Monastero.*

As I wander uphill to the main road in Bellagio, *Via Giuseppe Garibaldi*, I find myself at the town hall, or municipio, on the right side. To the left is a paved footpath that has a tiny sign saying *Salita Cappuccini*. This is the way to Pescallo.

From here the walking is all downhill and mostly on steps and paths made of dirt. Pescallo is not even ten minutes away but having to traverse the treacherous path makes it seem further. I keep wondering how many more steps can there be, because as soon as I turn a corner, there seem to be another thirty steps or so. I will likely not forget walking down *Vicolo Strecchetta* for as long as I live. The steps are very steep, so this would not be a good walk for someone who is not in halfway decent physical condition. Not that I am a fitness freak, but I don't have trouble handling steep staircases. Finally, after turning right onto *Via E. Sfrondrati,* I am in Pescallo.

Pescallo truly looks like a picture on a postcard and is an enchanting little fishing community. Ducks swim near the shoreline. A young couple sits on a bench near me. They seem to enjoy the scenery as I do. I like the view of the colorful boats pulled up on the shore. This could be a scene out of a romantic movie.

There are only two hotels in Pescallo; one, *La Pergola,* is operated by a family. It sits along the lake and has a great, covered outdoor restaurant. Originally a fourteenth-century convent, it now attracts guests who appreciate the tranquility and beauty of the area. Experiencing Pescallo is the epitome of delighting in il dolce far niente.

Back in Bellagio I stop in for a cup of cappuccino at a café where free Wi-Fi is available. I make a Skype call and take care of a few other matters while I have the chance to be connected.

I really like Bellagio. After browsing and making some small purchases, I am now hungry. Several lakeside outdoor restaurants dot the lakeshore and I choose to have lunch at one of the outdoor cafés. I notice that most of the tourists speak English, and many of the shop owners and waiters here are fluent in both Italian and English. After lunch and some more sightseeing, I take the ferry back to Varenna. The views from the boat are again great opportunities for me to take another twenty digital shots of Varenna.

It does not rain on the way home, and I spontaneously decide to visit a cemetery on the other side of my hotel. Italian cemeteries are much different from most in the U.S., especially since they frequently include a photo of the deceased on the monument. These spur-of-the-moment decisions are added benefits to independent travel without a rigid agenda.

After returning to the hotel I am happy to have time to sit out on the terrace again for several hours and do some writing, totally enjoying the quiet and lack of any schedule.

This last morning in Varenna, I indulge in one more breakfast on the pretty terrace overlooking the lake, pay my bill, and take a taxi to the small Varenna train station. Here, I wait outside with some other Americans who are also leaving Hotel Eremo Gaudio. We talk about how much we love Italy and compare notes about our recent adventures.

Geneva

I am on my way to Geneva, Switzerland, to visit my uncle and my cousin for three days. Uncle Sam is also my godfather and will be eighty-nine next week. I remember receiving a beautiful European, hand-painted jewelry box from him when I was a child, but my memory of his living in the States is dim.

Each time I travel to Italy, he invites me to visit. Since I have an extended vacation this trip, I am happy to include a few days in Geneva. Uncle Sam and his daughter, Clare, live together, and for the past two years, another person, Johanna, also lives with them at their flat. Johanna is a longtime friend of Clare's, and now she is a caregiver for both my uncle and my cousin, because they both need some assistance.

Although I am excited to see some of my extended family after traveling away from home for the past two and a half months, I feel a little uneasy and nervous today. I am going to a different country for the first time on this trip, and I do not speak French or know how to read the French signs. In Italy I feel very comfortable communicating in another language, but today my travels take me to a place where I feel out of my comfort zone. It helps that I will not be on my own once I arrive at my uncle's. This day is an adventure.

The train from Varenna arrives at the Milan train station after an hour. I do not have to wait long before my train for Geneva departs the station. For the four-hour train ride I have a ticket for a window seat in first class, the only choice open to me. I anticipate a beautiful long ride through the Alps to Geneva.

Unfortunately things are not happening as planned. Not long after I board the train and am comfortably seated, the conductor appears and informs me that this train is no longer going to Geneva. Instead I must switch trains after two stops. Apparently the Simplon Tunnel is still closed due to last Thursday's fire, and this requires some shuttling of trains. In *Domodossola* I will have to take a train to Switzerland, where I need to ask the Swiss authorities how to proceed from there.

This outlook is more than a little stressful for me because I have no idea of the names of towns in Switzerland. I also do not speak French or German, nor do I have a Swiss map. I gather enough information from a few other English-speaking passengers to understand that all passengers must get off this train and switch to one to *Brig*, the first stop in Switzerland. After that we will have to find the train going to our original destinations.

On the second train I have the good fortune to meet a young Australian teacher named Emma, who has been living in Florence for the past two months. We both are destined for Geneva, so we provide moral support for each other in finding our way to the next train. She is on her way to her cousin's wedding in France and has been dragging her brother's extra bag along to do him a favor. Of all times my phone does not seem to work, so Emma is kind enough to let me use her cell phone. I am able to notify Johanna of the train changes. She is supposed to meet me at the railroad station in Geneva,.

Along the route I enjoy the sights in the countryside, especially a few castles and some snow on the high peaks of the Alps. I definitely know that I am no longer in Italy because the house designs appear completely different. Here, the chalet-style roofs very much resemble what I have seen in mountain towns in the western United States. Even though these mountain home styles are attractive, I prefer the housing modes in most of Italy.

Soon the weather changes to rain which continues for most of the trip, so my expectation of a beautiful ride through the Alps turns into a disappointment.

As the train approaches Geneva, I become aware that the city has two stations, the main train depot and the station at the airport. I assume the one I want is the main station, so that is where I disembark, an hour after the scheduled time.

Johanna is not waiting on platform number three, as expected, and I am on my own with no phone. I ask a stranger, who fortunately speaks English, if I may use her phone to call Johanna. I offer to pay her since she initially seems hesitant, but then she offers me the phone. Is she agreeable because I appear to be an American tourist who is desperate? I am sure my anxiety is apparent, since I feel so nervous about the whole situation. "Thank you," I say in English, hoping she understands. I feel so grateful to this kind person for loaning me her phone.

Fortunately I reach Johanna after dialing the number I have for her. She explains that she is here but at a different platform, so within a minute or two, we find each other. Johanna walks up to me holding an 8½ by 11 inch paper with my photo on it. She walks toward me on the platform and says, "The photo does not look like you. Your hair is longer." What she says is true, so I understand the confusion. In a country where I feel like a fish out of water, I am relieved that we finally encounter each other.

Johanna seems so kind, greeting me with a big smile. I like her immediately. Her car is parked not too far from the station. We store my baggage and drive the short distance to the village of *Grand Lancy*, home of my uncle. He greets me with arms outstretched.

"Welcome, Margie! You have not changed since I saw you in Cleveland four years ago," he says, adding, "Dinner is almost ready." I am amazed to learn that he cooks. He hands me a glass of wine, "Try this while I get ready to serve and join you." I feel so good to be with family. Suddenly the day is looking much better.

The next morning I know I am not in Italy, but I feel happy waking up in a house with family around. Clare is a joy; I like her positive attitude despite her disability. I am glad to have a chance to get to know Johanna first-hand, rather than hear stories about her. She is Swiss-German but speaks perfect English, a talent I will later appreciate when we go shopping together. Switzerland is not on the euro currency but on the Swiss franc, and of course I have no clue how to calculate the exchange rate.

On this rainy day, the four of us spend most of the time inside. We enjoy catching up on family stories. For lunch I am treated to a French meal of *Vol-au-vent*, which means "gone with the wind," named for its light puff pastry. This tasty dish is made with mushrooms in a cream sauce and a little meat. Combined with the flaky pastry shell, the flavor is absolutely fantastic. I am also fortunate to taste some real Gruyère cheese as well as some Camembert; I discover that I prefer the Gruyère.

What a treat to be able to have my laundry done in a house with a real washer and a dryer! Sometimes the little things mean the most. After almost three months of doing laundry mostly by hand in a sink, I really appreciate this bonus. I am more than happy to do it myself, but my uncle insists on doing it for me. He is amazing!

While I am here, I hope to interview him and record his voice, at the request of my son, Brian, who is a sound recordist and sound mixer by profession. He values the chance to hear an oral family history and record it forever. Uncle Sam is a retired engineer and an inventor, so Brian is curious, as am I, to hear him talk about his inventions. Today seems to be a good time for my uncle. We decide to go to his office, where there is the least amount of noise, to record whatever he is willing to discuss.

For just under thirty minutes Uncle Sam talks to me about his inventions. He particularly mentions his experience in tweaking the invention of 3-D television without the use of glasses, as well as the involved process of obtaining a patent. He also shares some details about another invention but explains that he is not quite finished with that one. "You've got to solve problems before you go to the next one," he says, sharing his wisdom. I am grateful that he is willing and able to grant me this live interview.

Although I don't realize it now, this will turn out to be my last visit with my uncle. A little more than a year later, and not long after he celebrated his ninetieth birthday, my Uncle Sam died following a heart attack. I am so grateful for the opportunity to spend time with him, and to be able to record his words. Thank you, Brian, for encouraging me to do this.

On Sunday, Clare and Johanna invite me to attend church services with them. I usually try to go to the Catholic Mass whenever I can on Sunday. In Italy, there is a church practically on every corner or in every piazza. Here the Catholic Church is not so close, nor is the time of Mass convenient, so I decide to go with Johanna and Clare to their church.

My first experience at a Pentecostal service is a positive one. Everyone I meet is very friendly and welcoming, and the service is in English. I enjoy it and am glad that I can share this event with my cousin and Johanna today. They are long-time members of this congregation, so they are also pleased to see that I like the service.

Afterward we drive to a French restaurant where Clare's older brother, Christopher, and Uncle Sam wait for us. I love seeing Chris as an adult for the first time. Even though he has Down's syndrome, he is quite functional, but he does not remember me. He lives in a nearby group home with others who are also developmentally challenged. At the restaurant I have one of the best desserts ever, a type of to-die-for apple pie à la Mode, which is like nothing I know from the States. Again my uncle is very generous, insisting on paying the entire bill.

"Thank you, Uncle Sam, for the unforgettable meal and conversation."

"You're welcome, Margie. I wish we did not have an ocean separating us..."

After lunch we return to the house and take some family photos. Then, Clare, Johanna, and I say goodbye to Chris and Uncle Sam, as we leave to visit some attractions.

I want to see the United Nations building, and Clare and Johanna want to drive to Lake Geneva, to show me the sights. We stop to photograph the UN building and head toward the lake, also called *Lake Léman*. Finding a parking spot on a Sunday takes time, but soon we walk all around this huge gorgeous body of water. Clare gets around on a mobility scooter, and she is thrilled to be out sightseeing. It is a perfect, sunny day, and flowers are in bloom almost everywhere I look. The fresh air is filled with an aromatic bouquet. One of our first stops while leisurely strolling near the lake, is one of Geneva's landmarks, the Flower Clock, located at the English Garden. The clock's second hand is almost eight feet long, making it the largest in the world. Clare says that this is one of Geneva's most famous attractions.

Of course, the other landmark, which can be seen from almost anywhere on the Geneva side of the lake, is the *Jet d'Eau*, the famous fountain, that can reach heights of 459 feet and pump 132 gallons of water per second. The wind blows some of the water sideways, and people who stand near this huge vertical jet of water are sprayed with the mist, but they don't seem to mind. It probably feels refreshing on such a warm day! The only times the fountain is shut off is on days when there are strong winds, the temperature dips below two degrees Centigrade, and for three weeks in November for maintenance.

On the other side of the lake is a beautiful rose garden where we walk at leisure and breathe in the fragrant air. I thoroughly enjoy spending the day outside with Clare and Johanna, laughing and taking photos of each other and of the landmarks. After more than two months of solo travel, to be able to spend this time with my family in Geneva, as well as see some of the sights, is great.

"Geneva is not a good example of the Swiss culture," explains Clare, "since it is such a cosmopolitan city. With the

United Nations, the World Health Organization, in addition to quite a few other international organizations here, a large number of people living in our city hail from other countries." Clare means that I am not truly seeing Switzerland by only visiting Geneva.

Tomorrow I leave for *Courmayeur*, a ski town in Italy at the foothills of *Mont Blanc*. This particular town is not so easy to reach from Geneva due to the fact that roads wind around mountains. At my uncle's home, I probably spend several hours trying to figure out logistically the best way to get to Courmayeur from here. Finally I make arrangements via the internet to leave from Geneva Airport on a bus to the French ski resort of *Chamonix*. The bus company, *ChamExpress,* advertises frequent trips for twenty-nine euros one way. From Chamonix a smaller shuttle bus of a different company provides transportation for the remaining trip through the Mont Blanc tunnel to Courmayeur.

I say *Au revoir* to my uncle and Clare. Johanna generously drives me to the airport. Once inside, I am a bit apprehensive while I wait for the bus to show up at the assigned place. Eventually my fears ease as an English-speaking agent of the bus company assures me that they have my reservation. All goes according to plan. On the ride to Chamonix I drink in the scenery to remember it.

When the bus arrives in Chamonix, I notice what a pretty skiing mecca it is. I recall hearing people speak of this location as being more popular than Courmayeur. Since my travel goals for this trip focus on Italy, Cormayeur is my destination of choice. After I depart the bus in Chamonix, I quickly find the ticket office where I need to pick up my reservation for the shuttle to Courmayeur.

I realize that I have now a nearly four-hour wait. I see a bus, however, that appears to be a shuttle. On a whim, I ask the Italian bus driver if this might be the shuttle to Courmayeur, and he acknowledges that indeed it is. When I explain that I have a reservation for a later shuttle, and ask permission to take an earlier bus, he kindly directs me to the ticket office and tells me he will wait for me. Immediately I feel at home again with an Italian bus driver making such a nice gesture. The French woman in the ticket office is not pleased, but she makes the adjustment. So off I go to arrive in Courmayeur three or four hours ahead of my original plan. I smile as I am on my way back to Italy!

Back to Italy before Going Home

Although the ski season is over, hikers and mountain climbers come to Courmayeur because it lies at the foothills of Mont Blanc, the largest mountain in Western Europe. Neither hiking nor mountain climbing is my thing, but I appreciate the beauty of nature and mountain scenery, so I am here to relax in a tranquil setting.

In June the resorts are not fully occupied. I am pleasantly surprised when *Stefano*, the hotel desk clerk at *Cresta et Duc Hotel*, informs me of an upgrade to a superior room. I cannot believe the view I have from my accommodation on the top floor with a balcony. This is relaxation at its best!

Courmayeur is not that big, but is very charming with its alpine look. The town looks much different from any of the other Italian towns on this trip. Its name, chalets and French-named shops make it obvious that much French influence exists here. Many signs are in both Italian and French. The only thing separating Italy from France here is Mont Blanc.

Although the streets are on small hills, I am surprised that I am so tired and winded after a short walk. In an aha-moment I realize that Courmayeur is at an elevation of 4000 feet, and I feel the mountain altitude.

The scenery is impressive, especially the snow-capped peaks of Mont Blanc. Courmayeur reminds me of the ski towns of Vail and Aspen in Colorado, including the shops with prices for tourists.

One of the few towns in Italy without a train station, Courmayeur necessitates travel by bus. Stefano kindly prints out the best travel itinerary for when I leave Thursday to go to San Remo. This excursion requires a bus and four trains. I think to myself, where is my car? But I am used to complex travel arrangements now, because small villages off the beaten track are not that easy to reach.

Rather than have dinner at a restaurant, I stop at a small groceria and buy a home-made panini and an apple. Along with a few cookies, this is my dinner tonight. Shall I mention that I want gelato too?

I love the thought of doing nothing. The idea of riding the cable car to Chamonix is tempting; however, the cable ride that originates in Courmayeur is closed at this time. I understand that a neighboring village operates one to Chamonix, but I decide against it. I opt to relax in this peaceful town.

Courmayeur is situated at the same latitude as Montreal, Canada, so sunrise is at five thirty. I awaken to sunlight shining through my window, but I lazily roll over and go back to sleep. What a great feeling to know that I don't have to catch a train today. I spend part of the day writing on my balcony and later meander about the town, inhaling the fresh, dry mountain air.

In the center of town, inside a small office, I purchase my travel tickets to my next destination. One of the friendly agents prints out my bus ticket to Aosta and my train tickets to San Remo, an itinerary suggested by Stefano from my hotel. "*Grazie, signorina. Lo apprezzo,*" I say. Thank you, miss. I appreciate it.

The two young women in the office smile at me and at each other."*Prego. Buon viaggio.*" You're welcome. Safe travels.

Since I have free time to relax in Courmayeur, and I have a travel article to submit with a deadline, I need to find a place with a computer. My iPad is great but has some limitations when it comes to article submissions and the use of specific templates. Stefano informs me that I can use the public library, and he provides simple directions.

In small towns most monuments, public buildings, churches, shops, and restaurants are within walking distance. With Stefano's directions, I soon locate the library, which is open. Inside I inquire if I may use the internet and explain to the library clerk that I am a guest at a local hotel.

The friendly young clerk shows me the section for computer terminals. He indicates that the use of the internet is free. The computers are Macs and even though I have a couple of Apple products, namely my iPhone and iPad, this is my first experience with a Mac computer. None of the library personnel speak English, only Italian and French. After a little trial and error with the computer, I ask for help from two teenagers who are doing computer work at the next station. We are able to communicate well enough for them to advise me. After a few minutes, I am able to upload my article in time for the editor's deadline. Mission accomplished.

Back outside, on the quiet empty streets, I notice two hikers. They each carry a backpack, which looks as though it weighs fifty pounds. I am glad that hiking in these mountains is not on my agenda.

At the top of a hill in the center of town is the Church of Saint Pantaleon, an old church with an interesting Romanesque-style bell tower and clock. I am fascinated with the bell towers and clocks in Italy and spend time photographing this one from various angles until I reassure myself that I have the perfect shot.

Between the intermittent rain and the fact that I am here during the off-season, I feel somewhat bored. Probably two days here, rather than three, is plenty of time. I am a little homesick, ready to return to Florida anytime. I still want to visit San Remo, though, my last destination on this adventure.

In serious need of a pasta fix after five days without any, I head out of my hotel in search of a restaurant. I fear that I might go through withdrawal, unless I find some pasta soon. Of course, after a short five-minute walk down the hill, I locate a place that serves delicious pasta.

Pizzeria du Tunnel Ristorante has an outdoor, covered seating area as well as a restaurant inside. I choose a seat at an empty outside table and order a pizza. During my meal a gentleman walks over to me and starts a conversation. "*Buona sera, Signora*," he says.

"*Buona sera, Signore*," I say. "*Sei il proprietario?*" Good evening. Are you the owner?

"Yes, I am," he says in English and explains to me that he is originally from Napoli and in the restaurant business for over twenty years.

"*Tutto buono*," I say, letting him know how much I enjoy the meal. He is pleased. Afterward I climb back up the hill to return to my hotel, just in time before the rain starts.

On my last morning in this northern mountain town, the air feels cool. As I walk to the bus stop at six fifteen, I pull my jacket a little tighter. The rain is gone and the thermometer reads 50° F. The bus to Aosta arrives, right on schedule, to take me on my first leg of today's journey. The remainder of the day I spend in travel via four trains to arrive in San Remo in the afternoon. Everything works out smoothly. As I move closer to the seashore, I have a smile on my face.

From the modern San Remo train station, *Hotel Paradiso* is a short taxi ride away. When I arrive, my American friend, Tammy, is already in the lobby to greet me. Our desire to learn the Italian language from the same Italian teacher in Florida culminates in this shared time in Italy. How wonderful to have a friend with me during the last part of my travels here. Tammy is a frequent visitor to Italy, and on this trip she is traveling to various European locations.

"I'll check in and freshen up, Tammy," I say, "then we can take a look at this town. I feel like walking after sitting in all these trains. Does that sound all right?"

"Fine with me," she says.

One of the first landmarks we find is the historic 1913 Russian Orthodox Church on *Via Nuvoloni*. What separates this church from so many others, aside from it being Russian Orthodox, is the presence of soft music playing inside. Below the main floor we view a crypt that contains the remains of Montenegro royalty. Perhaps this is one reason that many Russian tourists visit here. Some of the local restaurants also cater to Russian visitors; their menus include the Russian language.

After our tour of the church, we continue our stroll through the shopping areas and happen upon an outdoor market. We also stop in to see several more churches, but do not linger long. On the next street we pass the famous San Remo Casino, which takes up an entire city block, but neither of us cares to go inside.

We make our way through the centro storico and notice some very old trees that Tammy thinks may be fig trees. We continue our uphill walk and meet a local Italian woman who proudly tells us in her language that she is eighty years old. "*Io sono ottant'anni.*" She certainly looks very fit as she lugs a shopping cart up the steep steps to her small home. I imagine that these steps are part of her daily routine and she thinks nothing of it. How dare I complain that my feet hurt as I climb stairs on a vacation? Once again I am keenly aware of the difficult lifestyle for those who dwell in these homes alongside the arduous staircases.

Finally we reach the high point of *Piazza San Costanza*, where we have panorama views of the city and down to the water. The climb in the heat is worth it after all. The centro feels cool and is a pleasant reprieve from the hotter temperatures below.

La Pigna is the oldest part of San Remo. No cars are allowed in this medieval area. The streets are not wide enough to accommodate vehicles, and the houses are built almost on top of one another. The only way to get to these homes is on foot, up and down the steep inclines and staircases. I love the quaintness of it all, but definitely would not be able to live here; the lifestyle is too hard.

We browse around some more and eventually find our way back to the seaside. By this time we are both hungry and glad to locate an outdoor trattoria that looks busy. "Let's give it a try," Tammy says. *Ristorante/Pizzeria Napul'è* turns out to be the perfect place for us to have dinner tonight. I am tempted to try the veal milanese, but because I am not able to fully understand exactly how the cook prepares the veal, I decide against it. Instead, I choose a pasta dish, but Tammy orders the veal. She offers a taste to me, and now I regret my decision to choose pasta.

"Tammy," I say, your breaded veal cutlet looks and tastes exactly like my Grandma Savoca's."

"Well, you came to Italy to experience some of the life your grandparents led. Food and drink play an important role in any culture."

"You are right," I say and grin. "We may have to return here."

After our *revealing* dinner, we stroll along the boardwalk near the ocean to return to our hotel. The air feels so pleasant and the temperature is perfect. With a slight breeze off the water, I do not feel the humidity. Another factor about Italy I like very much.

Following yesterday's string of exhausting activities, Tammy and I take off for the shore today. Both of us are in the mood for a few hours of relaxation. Hotel Paradiso has an arrangement with a private beach, the *Euro Nettuno,* where hotel guests have free access to a sandy strand (yes, real sand), an umbrella, and chairs. Now I can completely relax. The rhythmic sound of the waves and the steady rays of the sun make me want to linger here until sunset.

Pre-arranged plans for the afternoon take precedence, however. Annemari, a friend of Tammy's, resides in

Villefranche, on the French Riviera. Since she likes to drive and does not live too far from here, Annemari intends to meet us this afternoon at our hotel. She wants to drive us into the hills above San Remo to explore the small villages there. So we benefit from a personal tour guide for the day, as I did in Cividale with Nerina, and in Milan with Angela. I am excited to see some out-of-the-way places most tourists never visit.

Annemari is friendly and gracious. I like her as soon as we meet. The three of us depart in her economy-size car for *Coldirodi* and discover that the roads are so narrow that we cannot even navigate them with her little car. A lot of the streets in these medieval villages were built prior to the automobile era. At that time people either walked everywhere or, perhaps, they used a donkey or mule for transportation. Although San Remo is very close to France, I have no doubt that I am in Italy.

As we drive higher toward *Monte Bignone*, we are treated to some beautiful panorama views of San Remo. Monte Bignone is at an elevation of over 4200 feet and, even so we are not going to the top of the mountain, we are not far below it. From here the view down to sea level from here is spectacular.

The area is just striking, and the air feels so much cooler once we reach altitudes of 2000 feet above sea level. These hill towns suddenly appear around a bend and I can see the whole town from a distance, which is great for a photographer like me. Ninety-nine percent of tourists to San Remo never have the chance to witness the beauty of nature from this vantage point. I appreciate the opportunity.

Next we drive through the town of *Bajardo* and then find the hilltop town of *Apricale*. The view of this town from a distance looks amazing. We get out of the car again to take more photos. Thank goodness, Annemari likes to shoot photos too, so she doesn't mind making the stops.

In Apricale we must park the car and walk into the pedestrian-only part of town. Here we find cobblestoned, steep and narrow walkways, called *caruggi*. A bit farther along, we end up at the main piazza and castle. Only a small number of other people are in the streets so I feel as though the three of us have this town all to ourselves.

In the main piazza, we are fascinated as we watch a few local men playing a game of handball. The more we observe them, the more it becomes apparent to us that this game is quite unique, in that it requires the use of a device worn on the wrist. This device is then used as each man hits the ball as hard as possible, aiming for a wall in a narrow alley. Other players hit it back, and someone keeps score, although I am not clear on how points are scored. A few spectators sit on a ledge above the piazza, others on benches below.

From one of the locals we learn that this game is called *Balu Ball*, also known as *Pallone Elastico*. And hear that there is a tournament every June and July, so this game may actually be a part of it. The players wear uniforms and seem to take the game *very* seriously. From what I understand, this game is unique to Apricale. Later, however, I learn that the game is also played in other areas of Liguria and the *Piemonte* region as well.

On the other side of the piazza stands a castle. We decide to take a self-guided tour for a nominal fee. The original castle is now a museum of a variety of items, but with a strong focus on the arts. As we walk through the castle and gardens surrounding it, our cameras record future memories along the way.

Throughout Apricale, walls are decorated with a lot of art; these murals were all painted in 1966. Each year in August, the town stages an outdoor theater event, which seems to be a big draw for artists and performers from surrounding areas, including Nice.

One thing I find interesting about Apricale is the number of roaming cats. They pop up everywhere but appear well fed. Without any cars on the narrow streets, the felines do not have to worry about getting run over. Many of the homes are decorated with paintings of cats.

As we walk back through the piazza, the Balu game continues. We have to wait a few minutes before we can pass, so as not to interfere with the game, or get hit by a ball. Now many more spectators sit on the ledge and cheer for the competing teams.

After we leave Apricale, we decide to drive through a larger town, *Isolabona,* and continue on to *Dolceacqua.* Annemari says, "We must stop there to photograph the castle in town."

Only a few towns in this area claim to have a castle, and Dolceacqua is one of them. "You'll see," she says.

Annemari is right. Nearing the village, we see the castle already from the road because of its location on the edge of the hillside. Another photo opportunity.

Dolceacqua seems similar to Apricale in that it too is built on a hill and the streets are made of cobblestones. The old bridge and ruins of the famous castle provide great subject matter for photos. All three of us find unique angles to capture the scene with our cameras. At a local outdoor shop we talk with the vendor about the hand-made items she sells.

"I'd like something cool to drink. How about you?" I say.

"Sure," Tammy says. We can stop at this small bar. Right, Annemari?"

"That's fine with me."

Refreshed, we head back to San Remo and agree to return to the *Ristorante/Pizzeria Napul'è* for dinner, thanks to our favorable experience the previous night. Tammy and I are sure that Annemari will like this place too, and we are right. This time I definitely order the veal milanese, which is absolutely delicious. During our meal we find ourselves forced to listen to two guys who wander around and try to sell roses to the customers. We are in a tourist area at an outside restaurant, so this is not unexpected. Melodic, live Italian serenades from an accordion player, however, make up for the minor annoyance of the flower vendors.

By ten thirty we are back at the hotel where we thank Annemari for her guidance and driving, and say our goodbyes to her.

After this busy but satisfying day, I decide not to go to Monaco tomorrow but to relax in San Remo instead.

This morning I am able to catch up on some writing and then spend the rest of the day at the beach with Tammy. The clear blue sky promises a perfect day. Tammy suggests a swim in the Mediterranean Sea. The water temperature is just right and feels so refreshing. I do not usually swim in the ocean, because I am respectful of the power of the waves, but at Euro Nettuno, a breakwater creates a calm sea close to shore and allows me to swim without fear.

Today is Saturday and the beach is very crowded—ideal for watching people. I notice that there are a lot of families with small children; it is nice to see both the *mammas* and *papàs*, and sometimes *nonni*, take care of them. The teenagers are playing a ball game in the water, similar to ping pong but without a net. Everyone seems happy to be at the beach with their families and friends.

Quite a few vendors meander around on the beach, selling anything from sunglasses to bandanas, to knock-off purses, to watches, to bubble machines, to jewelry, and even clothing. I am fascinated as I watch the strategy of two particular guys. They actually seem to be pretty good salesmen, because several people buy items from them.

One of the vendors is a young man who is selling clothing. His sales strategy is most interesting to me as I observe him interacting with prospective customers. He is very pleasant and seems to establish a relationship and make friends with an entire family, with no high pressure sales tactics. Soon he sits down with this family who actually try on different items over their beach clothes. He has a selection of shorts and tops mostly. To see this beach shopping activity is a first for me.

Not long afterward, another guy with a similar strategy approaches the same family; he is selling purses. He sits down, makes friends with them, and spends time in conversation with the man, maybe a husband. At the same time, the women of the family check out the merchandise and decide about the purses. I notice that the salesman actually, in a friendly gesture, places his hand on the man's knee a few times. One woman buys a purse, and everyone seems happy. This is one-stop shopping at the San Remo beach.

Later, when this guy passes by Tammy and me, he asks us whether we want anything from "Thomas's Boutique on the Beach." This is great free entertainment, as well as Italian entrepreneurship.

The man I really like to watch, though, is the one selling coconut. Fresh coconut is a popular refreshment in the summer in Italy. I am familiar with it from my visits to Milano and other places such as Siena, where it is sold along with sodas. Usually the coconut is in a refrigerated display with cold water flowing over it.

The coconut vendor carries a bucket of water and another container of fresh coconut. He has a megaphone attached to his belt with a pre-recorded announcement, alerting everyone about the coconut for sale, as he walks up and down the beach. Plenty of people are buying from him. At one point he stops short, because beachgoers surround him for the coconut.

This whole scene reminds me of a time when I took a Caribbean cruise to an island called Coco Cay. A waiter would walk up and down the beach and announce "Coco Loco" trying to sell a popular alcoholic beverage. I am amused by today's experience.

During the entire day at the beach I never hear anyone yell or argue. Most people, from what I can tell, are Italians; maybe they are at the beach for the weekend or a vacation. These hours at the San Remo beach are among some of the more fun occasions for me in Italy. I do not regret the choice to skip the day in Monaco.

For our last dinner in this city we decide to go to a little place Tammy chooses, *Maona Pizzeria*. We select a table with a view of the waterfront. The restaurant is owned by two brothers, one of whom is taking our orders, and says, "I have kept this business open for twenty-six years. My brother is the chef."

Soon after we order our pizzas, we are able to look into the kitchen through an open-air window. We see the chef and can hear him singing! On the tiny windowsill of the cucina, we spot fresh basil and Italian parsley growing in pots. The food the brothers serve cannot be any fresher. We end the evening with a walk back to Hotel Paradiso, and I have some gelato. Of course.

My last full day in Italy has arrived. Tammy and I say our farewells and promise to stay in touch.

At 11:15AM I board my last train in Italy. Departure is from the very modern San Remo station, and three and a half hours later I am in Milano. Holiday Inn Express near the airport is my last hotel accommodation before I fly home tomorrow. My excitement and enjoyment throughout this memorable three-month journey are still with me as I begin my return to Florida. But, to borrow Dorothy's words from *The Wizard of Oz*, "There's no place like home," I am ready to settle down for a while.

I plan to continue my blog, because I have plenty more to write, and in greater detail, about the Italian people, the regions, and the fifty towns and villages whose charm captivates me beyond these past twelve weeks.

Epilogue

Away from Italy, I reflect on impressions I found amusing while there. They were just some of the nuances of the Italian lifestyle and culture I observed that eventually grew on me after I had spent my initial weeks there.

It seems that it was more than a coincidence that no matter where I was, whenever I asked for directions, it was always "one hundred meters" down the road, or only *cinque o dieci minuti*, five or ten minutes. In reality, almost every time, the distance was at least twice, if not three times, the quoted amount. I smile as I write this, because at first I found this frustrating, but eventually I realized that all I had to do was to double the time or distance and they would probably be accurate.

On the flip side, drawing from the passion most Italians exuded, they also tended to exaggerate sometimes, particularly when it came to products or food items from their region. No matter where I was, someone would tell me that the gelato in that area was the best gelato, because the pistachios came from Bronte, where they were grown, or the lemons came from local trees. I was persuaded to try the prosciutto because it was homemade, and the same with the wine, olive oil, and other local specialties. The local residents I met were so proud of the products from their individual regions and maintained their identity with those places.

I felt encouraged, though, to have met people who took so much pride in their culture and lifestyle that they boasted about it whenever they had a chance. How refreshing to witness that cultural pride, compared with people who are complaining about their city, workplace, or living situation.

My solo travel still dominates my thoughts, such as my satisfaction with my ability to speak Italian. Even though I cannot say that I was completely fluent in that language while traveling, I did know enough to be able to communicate with the Italian people, and even carry on conversations in Italian during an hour-long taxi ride. I plan to continue the relationships with my Italian friends, and communicate in Italian on e-mail, Facebook, and Skype, so I do not lose what I have learned.

At times, I find that I think and talk to myself in Italian. I even think of Italian words when I play Scrabble. After three months, the benefits of total immersion into the Italian culture and language are clear to me now. My Italian teacher, Lori Samarin, was so right when she told me that, in addition to my lessons in Florida, I would learn much more by spending time in Italy.

I would never have been able to put my language lessons into practice without Cindy Norris's support of my request for a lengthy leave during a time of nursing shortage. Thanks to her backing, I took the trip of a lifetime.

One reason I did not feel alone while I was in Italy was the ability to stay connected with friends and family at home. It was so important for me to know that I could make a Skype call or do Face Time and see my family from four thousand miles away. It was worth all the research ahead of time: to be able to know how to make the connections, to be able to write, call, and do a video chat. Even ten years ago this would have been impossible.

After my return I attempted to make veal milanese. Despite my pounding the veal thin enough and following my grandmother's recipe, somehow my preparation did not result in as good a dish as I had eaten in San Remo. I sadly expect that it never will be either, although I will continue trying.

Frequently someone asks me if I think I would like to live in Italy. Although the idea may sound tempting, I absolutely know that life is much harder there, and as an American, I am too spoiled with the conveniences of life in the States. Three months in Italy have definitely given me more of an appreciation for those conveniences, and I am reminded of it every day.

Just four months after the eventful trip, I felt the urge to go back to Italy again. I made travel arrangements to return, maybe this time for a cruise. I really thought I wouldn't go back, but even my friends knew me better than I thought I knew myself. They kept asking me, when I would plan my next pilgrimage to Italy.

I have the answer now with no doubts in my mind. I will always return.

Since a part of me remains in Italy, the love affair continues.

About the Author

Margie Miklas is a writer, photographer, and critical-care nurse, who has a passion for travel, with a particular love of Italy. She writes travel articles for several websites as well as a monthly newspaper, *La Gazzetta Italiana*.

Margie works part-time in a cardiovascular intensive care unit, and is always seeking out opportunities to travel, especially to Italy. She lives in Port St Lucie, Florida, where she enjoys spending time with her twin granddaughters, going to the beach, and working in her garden.

Margie writes a blog, margieinitaly, where you can follow her adventures throughout Italy. *Memoirs of a Solo Traveler - My Love Affair with Italy* is Margie's first book, and it is based on her three month solo adventure in Italy.

Her next book, *My Love Affair with Sicily*, will be published in early 2014.

http://margieinitaly.wordpress.com/

http://margiemiklas.com/

Contact Margie at:

margieeee@comcast.net

https://twitter.com/MargieMiklas

http://www.facebook.com/margie.miklas

Made in the USA
San Bernardino, CA
24 August 2017